Cleveland 2021

A Baseball Companion

Edited by Steven Goldman and Bret Sayre

Baseball Prospectus

Craig Brown, Associate Editor
Robert Au, Harry Pavlidis and Amy Pircher, Statistics Editors

Copyright © 2021 by DIY Baseball, LLC.
All rights reserved

This book or any part thereof may not be reproduced or transmitted in any form or by any means, electronic or mechanical, including photocopying, recording, or by any information storage and retrieval system, without permission in writing from the publisher.

Limit of Liability/Disclaimer of Warranty: While the publisher and the author have used their best efforts in preparing this book, they make no representations or warranties with respect to the accuracy or completeness of the contents of this book and specifically disclaim any implied warranties of merchantability or fitness for a particular purpose. No warranty may be created or extended by sales representatives or written sales materials. The advice and strategies contained herein may not be suitable for your situation. You should consult with a professional where appropriate. Neither the publisher nor the author shall be liable for any loss of profit or any other commercial damages, including but not limited to special, incidental, consequential, or other damages.

Library of Congress Cataloging-in-Publication Data:
paperback
ISBN-13: 978-1-950716-39-5

Project Credits
Cover Design: Ginny Searle
Interior Design and Production: Amy Pircher, Robert Au
Layout: Amy Pircher, Robert Au

Baseball icon courtesy of Uberux, from https://www.shareicon.net/author/uberux

Ballpark diagram courtesy of Lou Spirito/THIRTY81 Project, https://thirty81project.com/

Manufactured in the United States of America
10 9 8 7 6 5 4 3 2 1

Table of Contents

Statistical Introduction v

Part 1: Team Analysis

Performance Graphs 3
2020 Team Performance 4
2021 Team Projections 5
Team Personnel 6
Progressive Field Stats 7
Cleveland Team Analysis 9

Part 2: Player Analysis

Cleveland Player Analysis 16
Cleveland Prospects 85

Part 3: Featured Articles

Cleveland All-Time Top 10 Players 99
    by Matthew Trueblood

A Taxonomy of 2020 Abnormalities 105
    by Rob Mains

Tranches of WAR 111
    by Russell A. Carleton

Secondhand Sport 117
    by Patrick Dubuque

Steve Dalkowski Dreaming 121
    by Steven Goldman

A Reward For A Functioning Society 125
    by Cory Frontin and Craig Goldstein

Index of Names 129

Statistical Introduction

Sports are, fundamentally, a blend of athletic endeavor and storytelling. Baseball, like any other sport, tells its stories in so many ways: in the arc of a game from the stands or a season from the box scores, in photos, or even in numbers. At Baseball Prospectus, we understand that statistics don't replace observation or any of baseball's stories, but complement everything else that makes the game so much fun.

What stats help us with is with patterns and precision, variance and value. This book can help you learn things you may not see from watching a game or hundred, whether it's the path of a career over time or the breadth of the entire MLB. We'd also never ask you to choose between our numbers and the experience of viewing a game from the cheap seats or the comfort of your home; our publication combines running the numbers with observations and wisdom from some of the brightest minds we can find. But if you *do* want to learn more about the numbers beyond what's on the backs of player jerseys, let us help explain.

Offense

We've revised our methodology for determining batting value. Long-time readers of the book will notice that we've retired True Average in favor of a new metric: Deserved Runs Created Plus (DRC+). Developed by Jonathan Judge and our stats team, this statistic measures everything a player does at the plate–reaching base, hitting for power, making outs, and moving runners over–and puts it on a scale where 100 equals league-average performance. A DRC+ of 150 is terrific, a DRC+ of 100 is average and a DRC+ of 75 means you better be an excellent defender.

DRC+ also does a better job than any of our previous metrics in taking contextual factors into account. The model adjusts for how the park affects performance, but also for things like the talent of the opposing pitcher, value of different types of batted-ball events, league, temperature and other factors. It's able to describe a player's expected offensive contribution than any other statistic we've found over the years, and also does a better job of predicting future performance as well.

The other aspect of run-scoring is baserunning, which we quantify using Baserunning Runs. BRR not only records the value of stolen bases (or getting caught in the act), but also accounts for all the stuff that doesn't show up on the back of a baseball card: a runner's ability to go first to third on a single, or advance on a fly ball.

Defense

Where offensive value is *relatively* easy to identify and understand, defensive value is ... not. Over the past dozen years, the sabermetric community has focused mostly on stats based on zone data: a real-live human person records the type of batted ball and estimated landing location, and models are created that give expected outs. From there, you can compare fielders' actual outs to those expected ones. Simple, right?

Unfortunately, zone data has two major issues. First, zone data is recorded by commercial data providers who keep the raw data private unless you pay for it. (All the statistics we build in this book and on our website use public data as inputs.) That hurts our ability to test assumptions or duplicate results. Second, over the years it has become apparent that there's quite a bit of "noise" in zone-based fielding analysis. Sometimes the conclusions drawn from zone data don't hold up to scrutiny, and sometimes the different data provided by different providers don't look anything alike, giving wildly different results. Sometimes the hard-working professional stringers or scorers might unknowingly inflict unconscious bias into the mix: for example good fielders will often be credited with more expected outs despite the data, and ballparks with high press boxes tend to score more line drives than ones with a lower press box.

Enter our Fielding Runs Above Average (FRAA). For most positions, FRAA is built from play-by-play data, which allows us to avoid the subjectivity found in many other fielding metrics. The idea is this: count how many fielding plays are made by a given player and compare that to expected plays for an average fielder at their position (based on pitcher ground ball tendencies and batter handedness). Then we adjust for park and base-out situations.

When it comes to catchers, our methodology is a little different thanks to the laundry list of responsibilities they're tasked with beyond just, well, catching and throwing the ball. By now you've probably heard about "framing" or the art of making umpires more likely to call balls outside the strike zone for strikes. To put this into one tidy number, we incorporate pitch tracking data (for the years it exists) and adjust for important factors like pitcher, umpire, batter and home-field advantage using a mixed-model approach. This grants us a number for how many strikes the catcher is personally adding to (or subtracting from) his pitchers' performance ... which we then convert to runs added or lost using linear weights.

Framing is one of the biggest parts of determining catcher value, but we also take into account blocking balls from going past, whether a scorer deems it a passed ball or a wild pitch. We use a similar approach—one that really benefits from the pitch tracking data that tells us what ends up in the dirt and what doesn't. We also include a catcher's ability to prevent stolen bases and how well they field balls in play, and *finally* we come up with our FRAA for catchers.

Pitching

Both pitching and fielding make up the half of baseball that isn't run scoring: run prevention. Separating pitching from fielding is a tough task, and most recent pitching analysis has branched off from Voros McCracken's famous (and controversial) statement, "There is little if any difference among major-league pitchers in their ability to prevent hits on balls hit in the field of play." The research of the analytic community has validated this to some extent, and there are a host of "defense-independent" pitching measures that have been developed to try and extract the effect of the defense behind a hurler from the pitcher's work.

Our solution to this quandary is Deserved Run Average (DRA), our core pitching metric. DRA seeks to evaluate a pitcher's performance, much like earned run average (ERA), the tried-and-true pitching stat you've seen on every baseball broadcast or box score from the past century, but it's very different. To start, DRA takes an event-by-event look at what the pitchers does, and adjusts the value of that event based on different environmental factors like park, batter, catcher, umpire, base-out situation, run differential, inning, defense, home field advantage, pitcher role and temperature. That mixed model gives us a pitcher's expected contribution, similar to what we do for our DRC+ model for hitters and FRAA model for catchers. (Oh, and we also consider the pitcher's effect on basestealing and on balls getting past the catcher.)

DRA is set to the scale of runs allowed per nine innings (RA9) instead of ERA, which makes DRA's scale slightly higher than ERA's. Because of this, for ease of use, we're supplying DRA-, which is much easier for the reader to parse. As with DRC+, DRA- is an "index" stat, meaning instead of using some arbitrary and shifting number to denote what's "good," average is always 100. The reason that it uses a minus rather than a plus is because like ERA, a lower number is better. Therefore a 75 DRA- describes a performance 25 percent better than average, whereas a 150 DRA- means that either a pitcher is getting extremely lucky with their results, or getting ready to try a new pitch.

Since the last time you picked up an edition of this book, we've also made a few minor changes to DRA to make it better. Recent research into "tunneling"—the act of throwing consecutive pitches that appear similar from a batter's point of view until after the swing decision point–data has given us a new contextual factor to account for in DRA: plate distance. This refers to the distance between successive pitches as they approach the plate, and while it has a smaller effect than factors like velocity or whiff rate, it still can help explain pitcher strikeout rate in our model.

Recently Added Descriptive Statistics

Returning to our 2021 edition of the book are a few figures which recently appeared. These numbers may be a little bit more familiar to those of you who have spent some time investigating baseball statistics.

Fastball Percentage

Our fastball percentage (FA%) statistic measures how frequently a pitcher throws a pitch classified as a "fastball," measured as a percentage of overall pitches thrown. We qualify three types of fastballs:

1. The traditional four-seam fastball;
2. The two-seam fastball or sinker;
3. "Hard cutters," which are pitches that have the movement profile of a cut fastball and are used as the pitcher's primary offering or in place of a more traditional fastball.

For example, a pitcher with a FA% of 67 throws any combination of these three pitches about two-thirds of the time.

Whiff Rate

Everybody loves a swing and a miss, and whiff rate (Whiff%) measures how frequently pitchers induce a swinging strike. To calculate Whiff%, we add up all the pitches thrown that ended with a swinging strike, then divide that number by a pitcher's total pitches thrown. Most often, high whiff rates correlate with high strikeout rates (and overall effective pitcher performance).

Called Strike Probability

Called Strike Probability (CSP) is a number that represents the likelihood that all of a pitcher's pitches will be called a strike while controlling for location, pitcher and batter handedness, umpire and count. Here's how it works: on each pitch, our model determines how many times (out of 100) that a similar pitch was called for a strike given those factors mentioned above, and when normalized for each batter's strike zone. Then we average the CSP for all pitches thrown by a pitcher in a season, and that gives us the yearly CSP percentage you see in the stats boxes.

As you might imagine, pitchers with a higher CSP are more likely to work in the zone, where pitchers with a lower CSP are likely locating their pitches outside the normal strike zone, for better or for worse.

Projections

Many of you aren't turning to this book just for a look at what a player has done, but for a look at what a player is going to do: the PECOTA projections. PECOTA, initially developed by Nate Silver (who has moved on to greater fame as a political analyst), consists of three parts:

1. Major-league equivalencies, which use minor-league statistics to project how a player will perform in the major leagues;
2. Baseline forecasts, which use weighted averages and regression to the mean to estimate a player's current true talent level; and
3. Aging curves, which uses the career paths of comparable players to estimate how a player's statistics are likely to change over time.

With all those important things covered, let's take a look at what's in the book this year.

Team Prospectus

Most of this book is composed of team chapters, with one for each of the 30 major-league franchises. On the first page of each chapter, you'll see a box that contains some of the key statistics for each team as well as a very inviting stadium diagram.

We start with the team name, their unadjusted 2020 win-loss record, and their divisional ranking. Beneath that are a host of other team statistics. **Pythag** presents an adjusted 2020 winning percentage, calculated by taking runs scored per game (**RS/G**) and runs allowed per game (**RA/G**) for the team, and running them through a version of Bill James' Pythagorean formula that was refined and improved by David Smyth and Brandon Heipp. (The formula is called "Pythagenpat," which is equally fun to type and to say.)

Next up is **DRC+**, described earlier, to indicate the overall hitting ability of the team either above or below league-average. Run prevention on the pitching side is covered by **DRA** (also mentioned earlier) and another metric: Fielding Independent Pitching (**FIP**), which calculates another ERA-like statistic based on strikeouts, walks, and home runs recorded. Defensive Efficiency Rating (**DER**) tells us the percentage of balls in play turned into outs for the team, and is a quick fielding shorthand that rounds out run prevention.

After that, we have several measures related to roster composition, as opposed to on-field performance. **B-Age** and **P-Age** tell us the average age of a team's batters and pitchers, respectively. **Payroll** is the combined team payroll for all on-field players, and Doug Pappas' Marginal Dollars per Marginal Win (**M$/MW**) tells us how much money a team spent to earn production above replacement level.

Next to each of these stats, we've listed each team's MLB rank in that category from first to 30th. In this, first always indicates a positive outcome and 30th a negative outcome, except in the case of salary—first is highest.

After the franchise statistics, we share a few items about the team's home ballpark. There's the aforementioned diagram of the park's dimensions (including distances to the outfield wall), a graphic showing the height of the wall from the left-field pole to the right-field pole, and a table showing three-year park factors for the stadium. The park factors are displayed as indexes where 100 is average, 110 means that the park inflates the statistic in question by 10 percent, and 90 means that the park deflates the statistic in question by 10 percent.

On the second page of each team chapter, you'll find three graphs. The first is **Payroll History** and helps you see how the team's payroll has compared to the MLB and divisional average payrolls over time. Payroll figures are current as of January 1, 2021; with so many free agents still unsigned as of this writing, the final 2021 figure will likely be significantly different for many teams. (In the meantime, you can always find the most current data at Baseball Prospectus' Cot's Baseball Contracts page.)

The second graph is **Future Commitments** and helps you see the team's future outlays, if any.

The third graph is **Farm System Ranking** and displays how the Baseball Prospectus prospect team has ranked the organization's farm system since 2007.

After the graphs, we have a **Personnel** section that lists many of the important decision-makers and upper-level field and operations staff members for the franchise, as well as any former Baseball Prospectus staff members who are currently part of the organization. (In very rare circumstances, someone might be on both lists!)

Position Players

After all that information and a thoughtful bylined essay covering each team, we present our player comments. These are also bylined, but due to frequent franchise shifts during the offseason, our bylines are more a rough guide than a perfect accounting of who wrote what.

Each player is listed with the major-league team that employed him as of early January 2021. If a player changed teams after that point via free agency, trade, or any other method, you'll be able to find them in the chapter for their previous squad.

As an example, take a look at the player comment for Padres shortstop Fernando Tatis Jr.: the stat block that accompanies his written comment is at the top of this page. First we cover biographical information (age is as of June 30, 2021) before moving onto the stats themselves. Our statistic columns include standard identifying information like **YEAR**, **TEAM**, **LVL** (level of affiliated play) and **AGE** before getting into the numbers. Next, we provide raw, untranslated

Fernando Tatis Jr. SS

Born: 01/02/99   Age: 22   Bats: R   Throws: R
Height: 6'3"   Weight: 217   Origin: International Free Agent, 2015

YEAR	TEAM	LVL	AGE	PA	R	2B	3B	HR	RBI	BB	K	SB	CS	AVG/OBP/SLG
2018	SA	AA	19	394	77	22	4	16	43	33	109	16	5	.286/.355/.507
2019	SD	MLB	20	372	61	13	6	22	53	30	110	16	6	.317/.379/.590
2020	SD	MLB	21	257	50	11	2	17	45	27	61	11	3	.277/.366/.571
2021 FS	SD	MLB	22	600	95	24	4	31	81	50	165	17	8	.263/.331/.499
2021 DC	SD	MLB	22	628	100	25	4	32	85	53	173	19	8	.263/.331/.499

Comparables: Darryl Strawberry, Bo Bichette, Ronald Acuña Jr.

YEAR	TEAM	LVL	AGE	PA	DRC+	BABIP	BRR	FRAA	WARP
2018	SA	AA	19	394	136	.370	3.0	SS(83): -1.9	2.4
2019	SD	MLB	20	372	118	.410	7.1	SS(83): 0.9	3.4
2020	SD	MLB	21	257	126	.306	0.7	SS(57): -5.5	0.9
2021 FS	SD	MLB	22	600	126	.318	1.7	SS -1	3.9
2021 DC	SD	MLB	22	628	126	.318	1.8	SS -1	4.0

numbers like you might find on the back of your dad's baseball cards: **PA** (plate appearances), **R** (runs), **2B** (doubles), **3B** (triples), **HR** (home runs), **RBI** (runs batted in), **BB** (walks), **K** (strikeouts), **SB** (stolen bases) and **CS** (caught stealing).

Following the basic stats is **Whiff%** (whiff rate), which denotes how often, when a batter swings, he fails to make contact with the ball. Another way to think of this number is an inverse of a hitter's contact rate.

Next, we have unadjusted "slash" statistics: **AVG** (batting average), **OBP** (on-base percentage) and **SLG** (slugging percentage). Following the slash line is **DRC+** (Deserved Runs Created Plus), which we described earlier as total offensive expected contribution compared to the league average.

BABIP (batting average on balls in play) tells us how often a ball in play fell for a hit, and can help us identify whether a batter may have been lucky or not ... but note that high BABIPs also tend to follow the great hitters of our time, as well as speedy singles hitters who put the ball on the ground.

The next item is **BRR** (Baserunning Runs), which covers all of a player's baserunning accomplishments including (but not limited to) swiped bags and failed attempts. Next is **FRAA** (Fielding Runs Above Average), which also includes the number of games previously played at each position noted in parentheses. Multi-position players have only their two most frequent positions listed here, but their total FRAA number reflects all positions played.

Our last column here is **WARP** (Wins Above Replacement Player). WARP estimates the total value of a player, which means for hitters it takes into account hitting runs above average (calculated using the DRC+ model), BRR and FRAA. Then, it makes an adjustment for positions played and gives the player a credit for plate appearances based upon the difference between "replacement level"—which is derived from the quality of players added to a team's roster after the start of the season–and the league average.

The final line just below the stats box is **PECOTA** data, which is discussed further in a following section.

Catchers

Catchers are a special breed, and thus they have earned their own separate box which displays some of the defensive metrics that we've built just for them. As an example, let's check out Yasmani Grandal.

YEAR	TEAM	P. COUNT	FRM RUNS	BLK RUNS	THRW RUNS	TOT RUNS
2018	LAD	16816	15.7	0.8	0.1	16.5
2019	MIL	18740	19.4	1.8	-0.1	21.1
2020	CHW	4830	3.7	0.3	-0.2	3.8
2021	CHW	14430	16.7	-0.6	1.0	17.1
2021	CHW	14430	16.7	0.4	1.0	18.0

The **YEAR** and **TEAM** columns match what you'd find in the other stat box. **P. COUNT** indicates the number of pitches thrown while the catcher was behind the plate, including swinging strikes, fouls and balls in play. **FRM RUNS** is the total run value the catcher provided (or cost) his team by influencing the umpire to call strikes where other catchers did not. **BLK RUNS** expresses the total run value above or below average for the catcher's ability to prevent wild pitches and passed balls. **THRW RUNS** is calculated using a similar model as the previous two statistics, and it measures a catcher's ability to throw out basestealers but also to dissuade them from testing his arm in the first place. It takes into account factors like the pitcher (including his delivery and pickoff move) and baserunner (who could be as fast as Billy Hamilton or as slow as Yonder Alonso). **TOT RUNS** is the sum of all of the previous three statistics.

Pitchers

Let's give our pitchers a turn, using 2020 AL Cy Young winner Shane Bieber as our example. Take a look at his stat block: the first line and the **YEAR**, **TEAM**, **LVL** and **AGE** columns are the same as in the position player example earlier.

Here too, we have a series of columns that display raw, unadjusted statistics compiled by the pitcher over the course of a season: **W** (wins), **L** (losses), **SV** (saves), **G** (games pitched), **GS** (games started), **IP** (innings pitched), **H** (hits allowed) and **HR** (home runs allowed). Next we have two statistics that are rates: **BB/9** (walks per nine innings) and **K/9** (strikeouts per nine innings), before returning to the unadjusted **K** (strikeouts).

Next up is **GB%** (ground ball percentage), which is the percentage of all batted balls that were hit on the ground, including both outs and hits. Remember, this is based on observational data and subject to human error, so please approach this with a healthy dose of skepticism.

BABIP (batting average on balls in play) is calculated using the same methodology as it is for position players, but it often tells us more about a pitcher than it does a hitter. With pitchers, a high BABIP is often due to poor defense or bad luck, and can often be an indicator of potential rebound, and a low BABIP may be cause to expect performance regression. (A typical league-average BABIP is close to .290-.300.)

The metrics **WHIP** (walks plus hits per inning pitched) and **ERA** (earned run average) are old standbys: WHIP measures walks and hits allowed on a per-inning basis, while ERA measures earned runs on a nine-inning basis. Neither of these stats are translated or adjusted.

DRA- (Deserved Run Average) was described at length earlier, and measures how the pitcher "deserved" to perform compared to other pitchers. Please note that since we lack all the data points that would make for a "real" DRA for minor-league events, the DRA- displayed for minor league partial-seasons is based off of different data. (That data is a modified version of our cFIP metric, which you can find more information about on our website.)

Shane Bieber RHP

Born: 05/31/95 Age: 26 Bats: R Throws: R
Height: 6'3" Weight: 200 Origin: Round 4, 2016 Draft (#122 overall)

YEAR	TEAM	LVL	AGE	W	L	SV	G	GS	IP	H	HR	BB/9	K/9	K	GB%	BABIP
2018	AKR	AA	23	3	0	0	5	5	31	26	1	0.3	8.7	30	47.3%	.278
2018	COL	AAA	23	3	1	0	8	8	48^2	30	3	1.1	8.7	47	52.0%	.227
2018	CLE	MLB	23	11	5	0	20	19	114^2	130	13	1.8	9.3	118	46.2%	.356
2019	CLE	MLB	24	15	8	0	34	33	214^1	186	31	1.7	10.9	259	44.4%	.298
2020	CLE	MLB	25	8	1	0	12	12	77^1	46	7	2.4	14.2	122	48.4%	.267
2021 FS	CLE	MLB	26	10	6	0	26	26	150	121	18	2.1	11.7	195	45.5%	.297
2021 DC	CLE	MLB	26	14	7	0	30	30	196.7	159	24	2.1	11.7	257	45.5%	.297

Comparables: Luis Severino, Danny Salazar, Joe Musgrove

YEAR	TEAM	LVL	AGE	WHIP	ERA	DRA-	WARP	MPH	FB%	WHF	CSP
2018	AKR	AA	23	0.87	1.16	61	0.9				
2018	COL	AAA	23	0.74	1.66	69	1.2				
2018	CLE	MLB	23	1.33	4.55	74	2.6	94.7	57.4%	26.2%	
2019	CLE	MLB	24	1.05	3.28	75	4.9	94.4	45.8%	30.8%	
2020	CLE	MLB	25	0.87	1.63	53	2.6	95.3	53.6%	40.7%	
2021 FS	CLE	MLB	26	1.04	2.44	64	4.4	94.7	50.0%	33.2%	44.2%
2021 DC	CLE	MLB	26	1.04	2.44	64	5.8	94.7	50.0%	33.2%	44.2%

Just like with hitters, **WARP** (Wins Above Replacement Player) is a total value metric that puts pitchers of all stripes on the same scale as position players. We use DRA as the primary input for our calculation of WARP. You might notice that relief pitchers (due to their limited innings) may have a lower WARP than you were expecting or than you might see in other WARP-like metrics. WARP does not take leverage into account, just the actions a pitcher performs and the expected value of those actions ... which ends up judging high-leverage relief pitchers differently than you might imagine given their prestige and market value.

MPH gives you the pitcher's 95th percentile velocity for the noted season, in order to give you an idea of what the *peak* fastball velocity a pitcher possesses. Since this comes from our pitch-tracking data, it is not publicly available for minor-league pitchers.

Finally, we display the three new pitching metrics we described earlier. **FB%** (fastball percentage) gives you the percentage of fastballs thrown out of all pitches. **WHF** (whiff rate) tells you the percentage of swinging strikes induced out of all pitches. **CSP** (called strike probability) expresses the likelihood of all pitches thrown to result in a called strike, after controlling for factors like handedness, umpire, pitch type, count and location.

PECOTA

All players have PECOTA projections for 2021, as well as a set of other numbers that describe the performance of comparable players according to PECOTA. All projections for 2021 are for the player at the date we went to press in early January and are projected into the league and park context as indicated by the team abbreviation. (Note that players at very low levels of the minors are too unpredictable to assess using these numbers.) All PECOTA projected statistics represent a player's projected major-league performance.

How we're doing that is a little different this season. There are really two different values that go into the final stat line that you see for PECOTA: How a player performs, and how much playing time he'll be given to perform it. In the past we've estimated playing time based on each team's roster and depth charts, and we'll continue to do that. These projections are denoted as **2021 DC**.

But in many cases, a player won't be projected for major-league playing time; most of the time this is because they aren't projected to be major-league players at all, but still developing as prospects. Or perhaps a player will provide Triple-A depth, only to have an opportunity open up because of injury. For these purposes, we're also supplying a second projection, labeled **2021 FS**, or full season. This is what we would project the player to provide in 600 plate appearances or 150 innings pitched.

Below the projections are the player's three highest-scoring comparable players as determined by PECOTA. All comparables represent a snapshot of how the listed player was performing at the same age as the current player, so if a

23-year-old pitcher is compared to Bartolo Colón, he's actually being compared to a 23-year-old Colón, not the version that pitched for the Rangers in 2018, nor to Colón's career as a whole.

A few points about pitcher projections. First, we aren't yet projecting peak velocity, so that column will be blank in the PECOTA lines. Second, projecting DRA is trickier than evaluating past performance, because it is unclear how deserving each pitcher will be of his anticipated outcomes. However, we know that another DRA-related statistic–contextual FIP or cFIP-estimates future run scoring very well. So for PECOTA, the projected DRA- figures you see are based on the past cFIPs generated by the pitcher and comparable players over time, along with the other factors described above.

If you're familiar with PECOTA, then you'll have noticed that the projection system often appears bullish on players coming off a bad year and bearish on players coming off a good year. (This is because the system weights several previous seasons, not just the most recent one.) In addition, we publish the 50th percentile projections for each player–which is smack in the middle of the range of projected production—which tends to mean PECOTA stat lines don't often have extreme results like 40 home runs or 250 strikeouts in a given season. In essence, PECOTA doesn't project very many extreme seasons.

Managers

After all those wonderful team chapters, we've got statistics for each big-league manager, all of whom are organized by alphabetical order. Here you'll find a block including an extraordinary amount of information collected from each manager's entire career. For more information on the acronyms and what they mean, please visit the Glossary at www.baseballprospectus.com.

There is one important metric that we'd like to call attention to, and you'll find it next to each manager's name: **wRM+** (weighted reliever management plus). Developed by Rob Arthur and Rian Watt, wRM+ investigates how good a manager is at using their best relievers during the moments of highest leverage, using both our proprietary DRA metric as well as Leverage Index. wRM+ is scaled to a league average of 100, and a wRM+ of 105 indicates that relievers were used approximately five percent "better" than average. On the other hand, a wRM+ of 95 would tell us the team used its relievers five percent "worse" than the average team.

While wRM+ does not have an extremely strong correlation with a manager, it is statistically significant; this means that a manager is not *entirely* responsible for a team's wRM+, but does have some effect on that number.

Part 1: Team Analysis

Performance Graphs

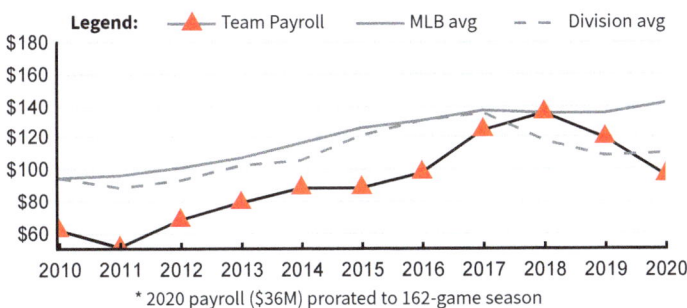

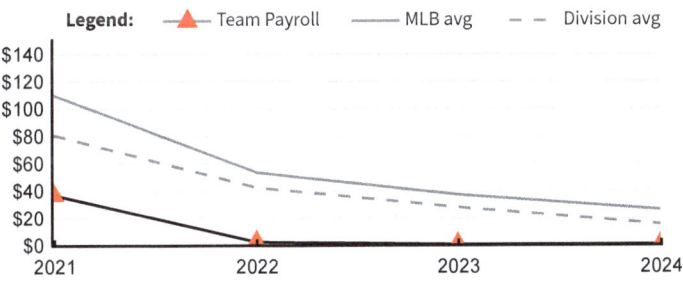

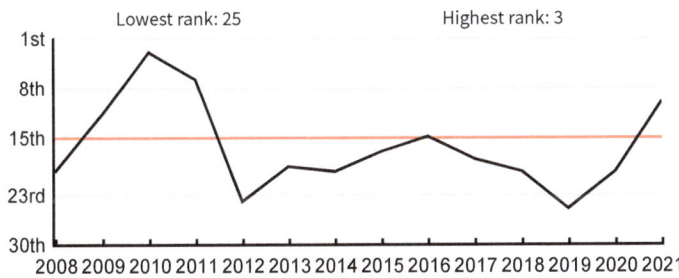

2020 Team Performance

ACTUAL STANDINGS

Team	W	L	Pct
MIN	36	24	0.600
CHW	35	25	0.583
CLE	**35**	**25**	**0.583**
KC	26	34	0.433
DET	23	35	0.397

dWIN% STANDINGS

Team	W	L	Pct
CLE	**30**	**30**	**0.506**
MIN	29	31	0.498
CHW	27	33	0.456
KC	24	36	0.403
DET	19	41	0.333

TOP HITTERS

Player	WARP
Francisco Lindor	1.4
Cesar Hernandez	1.1
José Ramírez	1.1

TOP PITCHERS

Player	WARP
Shane Bieber	2.6
Carlos Carrasco	1.3
Aaron Civale	0.9

VITAL STATISTICS

Statistic Name	Value	Rank
Pythagenpat	.576	8th
dWin%	.506	8th
Runs Scored per Game	4.13	25th
Runs Allowed per Game	3.48	1st
Deserved Runs Created Plus	97	16th
Deserved Run Average Minus	89	8th
Fielding Independent Pitching	3.51	1st
Defensive Efficiency Rating	.704	13th
Batter Age	28.6	13th
Pitcher Age	27.4	3rd
Payroll	$36.0M	25th
Marginal $ per Marginal Win	$1.1M	4th

2021 Team Projections

PROJECTED STANDINGS

Team	W	L	Pct	+/-
MIN	90.8	71.2	0.560	-6
With Nelson Cruz returning and Andrelton Simmons, J.A. Happ, and Alex Colomé on board the Twins seem like a balanced behemoth again.				
CLE	85.0	77.0	0.525	-9
That they've lost so many great players is an indictment of ownership. That they remain respectable is a testament to the agility of the front office.				
CHW	82.8	79.2	0.511	-11
Lance Lynn and Liam Hendriks give Tony La Russa the paint-by-numbers pitching staff he prefers, and all of the crucial cogs in last year's young lineup return.				
KC	71.5	90.5	0.441	1
Creeping back toward respectability, the Royals added reliable veterans coming off down years and will hope their youth movement gains momentum quickly.				
DET	65.7	96.3	0.406	3
The trend arrow is finally pointing up, but Robbie Grossman and Wilson Ramos qualifying as significant improvements shows they still have a long way to go.				

TOP PROJECTED HITTERS

Player	WARP
José Ramírez	3.9
Eddie Rosario	2.3
Franmil Reyes	2.3

TOP PROJECTED PITCHERS

Player	WARP
Shane Bieber	5.8
Zach Plesac	2.3
Aaron Civale	2.3

FARM SYSTEM REPORT

Top Prospect	Number of Top 101 Prospects
George Valera, #48	5

KEY DEDUCTIONS

Player	WARP
Francisco Lindor	3.7
Carlos Carrasco	3.2
Carlos Santana	2.2
Brad Hand	0.8
Adam Cimber	0.6

KEY ADDITIONS

Player	WARP
Eddie Rosario	2.3
Amed Rosario	0.8
Andrés Giménez	0.7
Jordan Humphreys	0.3

Team Personnel

President, Baseball Operations
Chris Antonetti

General Manager
Mike Chernoff

Assistant General Manager
Carter Hawkins

Assistant General Manager
Matt Forman

Assistant General Manager
Sky Andrecheck

Manager
Terry Francona

BP Alumni
Max Marchi
Ethan Purser
Keith Woolner

Progressive Field Stats

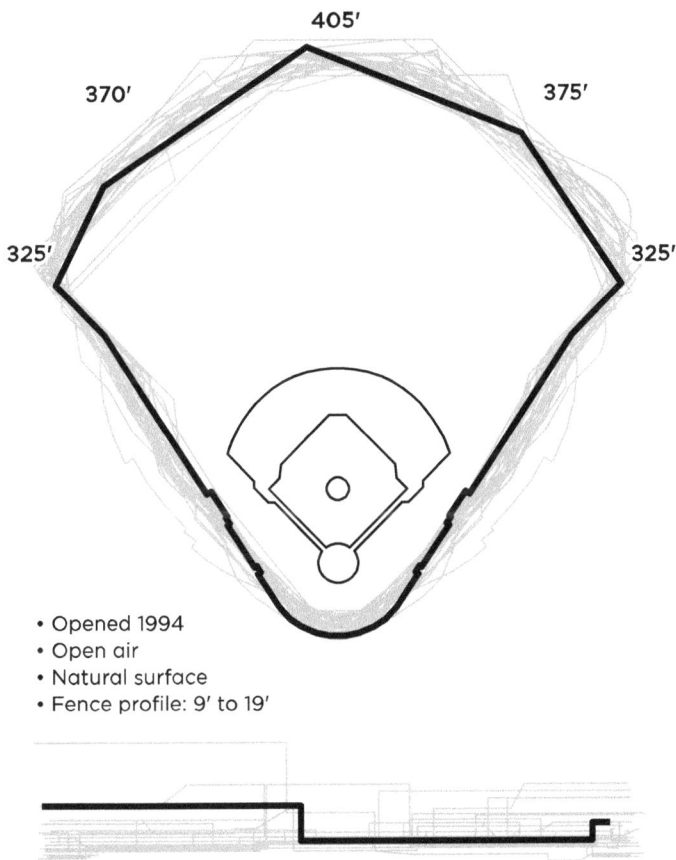

- Opened 1994
- Open air
- Natural surface
- Fence profile: 9' to 19'

Three-Year Park Factors

Runs	Runs/RH	Runs/LH	HR/RH	HR/LH
101	99	105	99	104

Cleveland Team Analysis

While the shortened 2020 MLB season will forever be linked with a pandemic, the underlying story is one of exceptionalism granted by baseball's status as America's pastime. Baseball has long enjoyed exemptions from the rules and social mores to which the vast majority of us must comply, and we can turn to a single week for Cleveland by way of illustration.

First, let's set the season's context. Although negotiations between MLB and MLBPA regarding financial obligations were contentious, all parties agreed that measures must be taken to protect the health of the players before pre-season activities resumed. It was generally understood that MLB would cooperate with epidemiologists and federal, state, and local public health authorities to provide evidence-based guidance to teams and players. Public health experts widely agreed that wearing a mask over our mouths and noses would reduce transmission of SARS-CoV-2. We also knew that maintaining physical distance from others—in particular, avoiding indoor spaces—would slow the spread of the virus. Accordingly, stadium facilities were reconfigured so as to allow for adequate ventilation and space between players. Facial coverings were strongly encouraged, while interactions with people outside of family, teammates, and MLB personnel were forbidden. These measures were deemed all the more critical given the risk of asymptomatic transmission.

Epidemiologists and virologists agreed that frequent testing was a critical tool for mitigating spread of the virus; however, across the United States, there was a lack of adequate diagnostic testing, with a constant shortage of laboratory reagents and long turnaround times. Major League Baseball equipped their partner Sports Medicine Research and Testing Laboratory with the equipment and consumables needed for PCR testing of thousands of league personnel each week. Anticipating public criticism, MLB pledged to offer free diagnostic and antibody testing to healthcare workers and first responders in team cities. This gesture of goodwill, coupled with the country's desire for a distraction during challenging times, contributed to the sentiment that MLB was doing its part to support communities.

Although there was a general consensus on how to slow the spread of the virus, little was known about the disease itself, and the prognosis and outcomes of COVID-19 were still not well understood. The long term ramifications of COVID-19 had yet to be ascertained. This point was made abundantly clear to MLB when the Red Sox' Eduardo Rodriguez became the exemplar of what could happen to a young, healthy athlete who developed COVID-19. Rodriguez tested positive for COVID-19 and was diagnosed with cardiac myocarditis, an inflammation of the heart muscle. It was rapidly determined that he would not play the 2020 season, but reports were hopeful that Rodriguez would recover quickly. However, it is not clear if the severity of his condition was widely known; follow up reports months later celebrated that Rodriguez was again able to walk unassisted, indicating that his condition was much more severe than previously reported.

One might think that seeing COVID-19 affect a contemporary in this way would have served as a warning to other baseball players who may have been concerned about their or their teammates' health. If fear did not suffice as motivation, surely the mandates in the MLB health and safety protocols would ensure compliance? Or perhaps embarrassment and shaming on social media would deter violators. Indeed, it was just such derision and backlash that resulted after Cleveland's first violation of MLB protocols: Just after the beginning of summer camp, outfielder Franmil Reyes posted photos of himself on social media where he wasn't wearing a mask. Reyes issued an apology for ignoring MLB protocols, and endangering both his teammates' health and the season.

As tenuous as it was, summer camp continued and the season began; less than two weeks later, starting pitchers Mike Clevinger and Zach Plesac chose to violate MLB health and safety protocols by visiting friends during an away series in Chicago.

On Saturday, August 8th, Plesac took the mound against the White Sox for his third start of the season. That same night, he opted to visit friends while in Chicago. The following day, his indiscretion was revealed, and he was sent home by car service to isolate him from his teammates. Initial comments from teammates expressed their disappointment but confidence that this would be handled internally.

As more details emerged, the story only grew worse: fellow starting pitcher Mike Clevinger had been out and about on Saturday as well. Not only did he lie, he did not confess when his teammate's night out was revealed. Clevinger defended Plesac, allowing him to bear the brunt of the judgement of a night out, letting Plesac stand alone and take the punishment for violating protocol. To top it all off, Clevenger flew home on the team plane on Sunday evening, potentially jeopardizing his teammates' health. Plesac's subsequent video confession, flaunting his decision to socialize and hide the truth upon returning to the team, threw salt in the wound.

Team chemistry is a nebulous concept, warmly embraced by some while harshly denied by others. When we speak of team chemistry, we usually speak of it as an additive, positive effect. But in the grand balance of the universe, it stands to reason that the positive cannot exist without the negative, and we should also consider that team chemistry can have a detrimental effect. When trust is breached and the bonds between teammates are fractured, it can have a deleterious effect.

Thus, it was no surprise when Cleveland players had harsh comments for their teammates. Francisco Lindor did not mince words: "At the end of the day, we have to sit and look ourselves in the mirror. And it's not about the person you see in the mirror—it's about who's behind you, the other people. It's not about that one person in general. It's about everybody around him and the family members that are behind us…We're in a time right now with COVID-19, with racism, everything. This is a time to be selfless. This is when we have to sit back and understand this is not about one person specifically. It's about everybody. You have to go out there and understand that it's about your neighbor and your neighbor's neighbors. It's not just you specifically."

Lindor's comments highlight the egregious violation that Plesac and Clevinger committed. The problem wasn't just that Clevinger and Plesac broke MLB COVID-19 protocols or ignored public health guidance; they had failed to consider the impact of their behavior on others—behavior that ultimately got Clevinger sent packing for 80 cents on the dollar. And it wasn't just their teammates on the field—Plesac and Clevinger violated the trust of their community. Their selfishness placed their team at heightened risk of catching a highly contagious virus—whether that team is Cleveland or the general public. By skirting the rules, Clevinger and Plesac sent an unambiguous message: they were above the rules which MLB had put into place, the same protocols that everyone else was expected to follow.

Plesac and Clevinger's behavior is emblematic of a larger issue, as this exceptionalistic attitude pervades MLB and its affiliated organizations. For most of the 2020 season, denizens of many states were subject to travel restrictions and quarantine mandates, but MLB was granted exemptions to bypass these local travel and quarantine requirements. The rest of the country waited in long lines for COVID-19 testing, only to wait up to a week for test results; meanwhile, professional athletes could skip the line and the wait. Further, MLB actively contributed to the strain of the testing infrastructure by using laboratory reagents for their own tests, and not testing community members who indirectly supported the return of the baseball season. Although they had initially promised to provide diagnostic and antibody testing to healthcare workers and first responders, investigative reporting revealed that the league neglected to follow through on its offers.

Major League Baseball's lackadaisical adherence to public health guidelines was not the only breach of community goodwill in 2020 or in years prior. Cleveland is as good an example of any in baseball, how a team that has benefitted from primacy granted to sports and business, and especially sports businesses acts more as a parasite than in a mutualistic manner. Baseball teams trade on cultural value, capitalizing on a built-in fan (consumer) base by trading in cultural value only to shirk their obligation to reinvest into that culture. Cleveland's payroll of late peaked in 2018, but was on the decline for a second consecutive season in 2020 despite notable holes in their outfield. Instead of making news by bringing in players to address those weaknesses, the team was instead making waves for all but announcing that their star shortstop wouldn't be with the team long term, as owner Larry Dolan stated "enjoy him while you can."

Dolan bought the team in 1999 for $323 million. As of April 2020, the franchise was valued by Forbes at $1.15 billion. Whether Lindor will live up to the contract he seeks and may ultimately receive is to be determined, but there's no doubt of his value to the fans in Cleveland, except perhaps in the minds of Dolan and his front office.

Further still, the league has disrupted the symbiosis between professional baseball and local communities by dismantling the minor league system and withdrawing from small town America. This isn't just a matter of a warm sentimental feeling; we may never know the entirety of the economic benefits the minor league system brought to these small towns, and the vacuum left behind as short season teams consolidate will inevitably lead to a loss of jobs in baseball and in the local hospitality industry.

Being a member of a community confers benefits, but in exchange, there is also a tacit understanding that we must be responsible members of the community. We rely upon the collective efforts of our neighbors to protect us, but we also take it upon ourselves to ensure that our individual actions do no harm. As members of a community, we wishfully believe that having a professional sporting organization unites us with shared experiences and hometown pride. By rooting for a team, we're not just supporting the team, but demonstrating our support for the city as well. But as much as the community may support its hometown teams, the reverse is simply not true. We offer MLB financial incentives and exemptions to laws in order to enjoin professional baseball to join our communities, but MLB seeks to reap these benefits without honoring the unspoken commitment to take accountability for their actions.

This one week in Cleveland's season is representative of the selfish desire to take advantage of the benefits provided by a community without also being mindful of how our actions impact said community. It's a form of exceptionalism exhibited by MLB as a whole, the same exceptionalism that characterized the American response to the pandemic. Clevinger and Plesac did not hold themselves accountable for their actions and their betrayal of their teammates, just as MLB has not held itself accountable for violating the goodwill generously provided by the communities in which it operates. We should not be surprised when we see that same exceptionalism in our sports teams, who somehow think that calls for racial equality and social justice, and yes, infectious disease prevention does not apply to them.

During the pandemic, we vigilantly maintain at least six feet of space between ourselves and others, but this physical distance heightens our awareness of the emotional distance we are creating. We worry that being too close together promotes the spread of the virus, and we also worry that not seeing our family, friends, and colleagues in person slowly wears away our humanity and connections. But our communities are based not on physical proximity, but out of our shared concern for our neighbors and our neighbor's neighbors well being, health, and safety. Community is its own chemistry, a sense of shared obligation and pride, a foxhole miles wide. It requires not just an obedience, but a sense of willingness, a declaration of playing for a team instead of for one's self.

Long after the novel coronavirus becomes a treatable condition, after vaccines are widely distributed, will we remember who thought they were the exception to the rules? Will we remember who in our community took action to protect others, or who failed to fulfil their promises and obligations to the community?

—*Stephanie Springer's writing has appeared in The Hardball Times and Baseball Prospectus.*

Katherine Acquavella, Mike Axisa, and R.J. Anderson, "Cleveland places Mike Clevinger and Zach Plesac on restricted list for breaking COVID-19 protocols", CBS Sports, August 11, 2020. https://www.cbssports.com/mlb/news/cleveland-places-mike-clevinger-and-zach-plesac-on-restricted-list-for-breaking-covid-19-protocols//p>

Paul Hoynes, "Cleveland Indians place right-handers Zach Plesac, Mike Clevinger on restricted list", Cleveland.com, August 11, 2020. https://www.cleveland.com/tribe/2020/08/cleveland-indians-place-right-handers-zach-plesac-mike-clevinger-on-restricted-list.html

Ricky O'Donnell, "The Cleveland Indians were right to blast their teammates for breaking Covid protocol", SB Nation, August 12, 2020. https://www.sbnation.com/mlb/2020/8/12/21365118/cleveland-indians-covid-protocol-partying-chicago-coronavirus

Zack Meisel, "Terry Francona, Chris Antonetti and Francisco Lindor on the state of the Indians", The Athletic, August 11, 2020. https://theathletic.com/1989753/2020/08/11/terry-francona-chris-antonetti-and-francisco-lindor-on-the-state-of-the-indians/

Bradford William Davis, "MLB promised free COVID-19 testing for essential workers. We're still waiting", New York Daily News, September 24, 2020. https://www.nydailynews.com/sports/baseball/ny-mlb-covid-testing-health-workers-20200924-lgrlvj4qjfh3pnudvixpgzqwbe-story.html

Part 2: Player Analysis

Cleveland 2021

PLAYER COMMENTS WITH GRAPHS

Ben Gamel LF
Born: 05/17/92   Age: 29   Bats: L   Throws: L
Height: 5'11"   Weight: 177   Origin: Round 10, 2010 Draft (#325 overall)

YEAR	TEAM	LVL	AGE	PA	R	2B	3B	HR	RBI	BB	K	SB	CS	AVG/OBP/SLG
2018	TAC	AAA	26	94	19	8	3	1	16	10	12	4	0	.349/.415/.554
2018	SEA	MLB	26	293	37	14	4	1	19	31	60	7	3	.272/.358/.370
2019	MIL	MLB	27	356	47	18	0	7	33	40	104	2	2	.248/.337/.373
2020	MIL	MLB	28	127	13	8	1	3	10	13	39	0	2	.237/.315/.404
2021 FS	CLE	MLB	29	600	59	24	3	13	61	57	169	5	3	.234/.313/.370

Comparables: Jason Grabowski, Eric Valent, Danny Walton

Gamel was one of the great line-drive machines in baseball in 2020, with a league-leading 60 percent of his batted balls carrying a launch angle between 0 and 30 degrees. Unfortunately, he managed that in conjunction with the sudden, disastrous spike in strikeout rate he'd begun in 2019. A patient hitter, he got slightly more aggressive, but he guessed wrong too often and his swing became grooved. Pitchers predictably found the holes. He also dealt with a balky quadriceps muscle all year, resulting in an alarming loss of speed that further limited him. In 2021, his challenges will be to avail himself of good health by continuing to square up the ball—and to make more contact on the edges of the zone.

YEAR	TEAM	LVL	AGE	PA	DRC+	BABIP	BRR	FRAA	WARP
2018	TAC	AAA	26	94	135	.394	2.5	LF(8): -0.7, CF(6): -0.1, RF(1): -0.3	0.6
2018	SEA	MLB	26	293	98	.350	3.3	LF(48): -1.4, RF(40): -1.9, CF(4): 0.5	0.7
2019	MIL	MLB	27	356	81	.347	0.5	LF(70): -1.6, RF(23): 0.0, CF(22): -0.3	0.1
2020	MIL	MLB	28	127	82	.333	-1.9	RF(27): -2.0, CF(11): -0.9, LF(1): 0.1	-0.3
2021 FS	CLE	MLB	29	600	86	.316	0.1	LF 0, RF 0	0.5

Ben Gamel, continued

Batted Ball Distribution

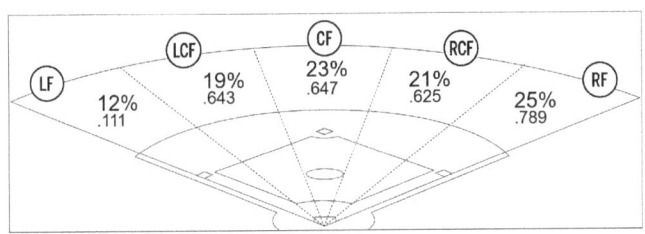

Strike Zone vs LHP

Strike Zone vs RHP

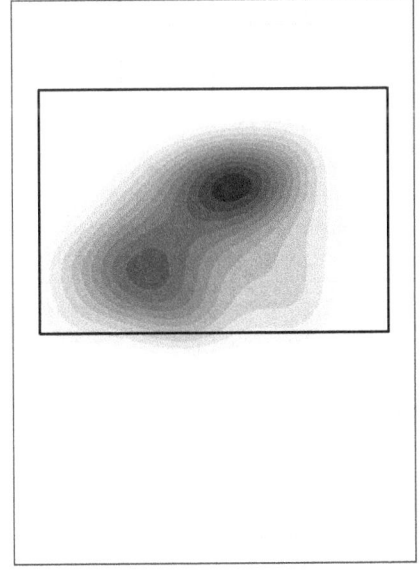

Cleveland 2021

Andrés Giménez SS

Born: 09/04/98   Age: 22   Bats: L   Throws: R
Height: 5'11"   Weight: 161   Origin: International Free Agent, 2015

YEAR	TEAM	LVL	AGE	PA	R	2B	3B	HR	RBI	BB	K	SB	CS	AVG/OBP/SLG
2018	STL	HI-A	19	351	43	20	4	6	30	22	70	28	11	.282/.348/.432
2018	BNG	AA	19	153	19	9	1	0	16	9	22	10	3	.277/.344/.358
2019	BNG	AA	20	479	54	22	5	9	37	24	102	28	16	.250/.309/.387
2020	NYM	MLB	21	132	22	3	2	3	12	7	28	8	1	.263/.333/.398
2021 FS	*CLE*	*MLB*	*22*	*600*	*65*	*27*	*3*	*13*	*65*	*34*	*138*	*17*	*9*	*.244/.308/.383*
2021 DC	*CLE*	*MLB*	*22*	*444*	*48*	*20*	*2*	*10*	*48*	*25*	*102*	*12*	*7*	*.244/.308/.383*

Comparables: Carter Kieboom, Franklin Barreto, José Iglesias

Giménez lost a bit of his luster when selling out for power in 2019, seeing an overall decrease in offensive production. So it was something of a surprise when he opened up the 2020 season as a member of the gameday roster, initially serving as a speed-and-defense complement to Robinson Canó, who possessed neither. By the end of the season, it quickly became clear that he had surpassed incumbent shortstop Amed Rosario in virtually every facet of shortstop play, and getting more comfortable with his swing has at least partially rectified the mistakes of his down season in Binghamton. No longer a rookie, Giménez's profile is back to where it was at the peak of his prospect powers: a do-it-all shortstop without a key carrying tool, but with above-average skills across the board. A useful player that is more than the sum of his parts, now all he needs is everyday playing time at the highest level to tease out if his ultimate role will be second-division starter, or perhaps something more dynamic. He'll get that time in Cleveland as the centerpiece of the trade that saw Francisco Lindor and Carlos Carrasco head to Flushing.

YEAR	TEAM	LVL	AGE	PA	DRC+	BABIP	BRR	FRAA	WARP
2018	STL	HI-A	19	351	112	.343	3.4	SS(83): 14.2, 2B(2): -0.1	3.1
2018	BNG	AA	19	153	100	.330	1.2	SS(36): -1.3, 2B(1): 0.2	0.4
2019	BNG	AA	20	479	91	.306	-2.9	SS(112): -0.7	1.3
2020	NYM	MLB	21	132	94	.318	0.6	SS(23): -2.5, 2B(19): 0.1, 3B(10): 0.2	0.1
2021 FS	*CLE*	*MLB*	*22*	*600*	*87*	*.304*	*1.5*	*SS 0, 2B 0*	*1.0*
2021 DC	*CLE*	*MLB*	*22*	*444*	*87*	*.304*	*1.1*	*SS 0*	*0.7*

Andrés Giménez, continued

Batted Ball Distribution

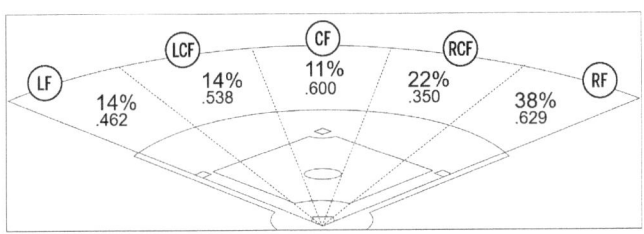

Strike Zone vs LHP   Strike Zone vs RHP

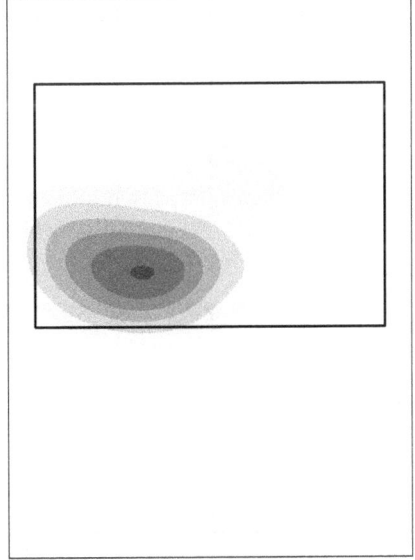

Cleveland 2021

Austin Hedges   C
Born: 08/18/92   Age: 28   Bats: R   Throws: R
Height: 6'1"   Weight: 223   Origin: Round 2, 2011 Draft (#82 overall)

YEAR	TEAM	LVL	AGE	PA	R	2B	3B	HR	RBI	BB	K	SB	CS	AVG/OBP/SLG
2018	ELP	AAA	25	31	7	3	0	3	11	3	9	0	0	.407/.452/.852
2018	SD	MLB	25	326	29	14	2	14	37	21	90	3	0	.231/.282/.429
2019	SD	MLB	26	347	28	9	0	11	36	27	109	1	0	.176/.252/.311
2020	SD	MLB	27	71	7	1	0	3	6	6	18	1	1	.158/.258/.333
2020	CLE	MLB	27	12	0	0	0	0	0	0	5	0	0	.083/.083/.083
2021 FS	CLE	MLB	28	600	67	22	1	23	68	40	174	2	2	.212/.274/.383
2021 DC	CLE	MLB	28	247	27	9	0	9	28	16	71	0	1	.212/.274/.383

Comparables: Humberto Cota, Ron Karkovice, Jesus Flores

Hedges' work with leather confronts the viewer with their own perceptions, forcing them to consider the very nature of the strike zone and the intersection between catcher and umpire. He blurs the distinction between ball and strike, often turning the former into the latter with skillful and wilful manipulation of space. It's a nice contrast from his lackluster work with the lumber, which makes it hard to go all Aldous Huxley with things. But behind the plate? Oh, behind the plate the artist embeds us in the constant conflict between command and chaos and the imagined and the real, leaving the observer to wonder what other dualities can exist.

YEAR	TEAM	P. COUNT	FRM RUNS	BLK RUNS	THRW RUNS	TOT RUNS
2018	SD	12042	13.0	0.1	-0.4	12.7
2019	SD	13488	26.0	1.5	0.3	27.8
2020	SD	2971	1.7	0.4	0.0	2.1
2020	CLE	585	0.4	0.2	0.0	0.5
2021	CLE	9620	10.4	1.3	0.2	11.8
2021	CLE	9620	10.4	0.8	0.2	11.3

YEAR	TEAM	LVL	AGE	PA	DRC+	BABIP	BRR	FRAA	WARP
2018	ELP	AAA	25	31	151	.500	0.0	C(6): 0.5	0.3
2018	SD	MLB	25	326	88	.280	-2.1	C(83): 11.8	2.1
2019	SD	MLB	26	347	61	.228	0.9	C(95): 28.2, 3B(2): -0.0	2.9
2020	SD	MLB	27	71	75	.162	0.0	C(28): 0.5	0.3
2020	CLE	MLB	27	12	73	.143		C(6): -0.0	0.0
2021 FS	CLE	MLB	28	600	75	.266	-0.6	C 22, 3B 0	2.8
2021 DC	CLE	MLB	28	247	75	.266	-0.2	C 12	1.4

Austin Hedges, continued

Batted Ball Distribution

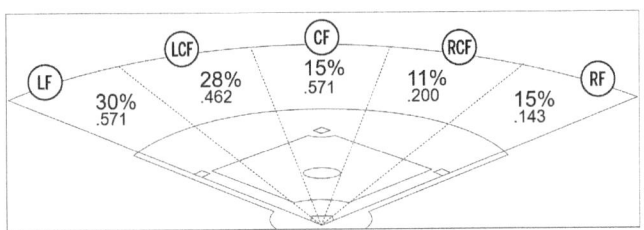

Strike Zone vs LHP   Strike Zone vs RHP

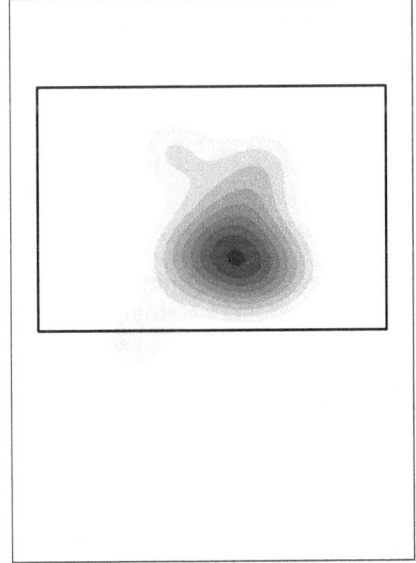

Cesar Hernandez 2B

Born: 05/23/90 Age: 31 Bats: S Throws: R
Height: 5'10" Weight: 195 Origin: International Free Agent, 2006

YEAR	TEAM	LVL	AGE	PA	R	2B	3B	HR	RBI	BB	K	SB	CS	AVG/OBP/SLG
2018	PHI	MLB	28	708	91	15	3	15	60	95	155	19	6	.253/.356/.362
2019	PHI	MLB	29	667	77	31	3	14	71	45	100	9	2	.279/.333/.408
2020	CLE	MLB	30	261	35	20	0	3	20	24	57	0	0	.283/.355/.408
2021 FS	CLE	MLB	31	600	81	26	2	12	54	62	133	12	6	.261/.345/.389
2021 DC	CLE	MLB	31	577	77	25	2	11	52	60	128	12	6	.261/.345/.389

Comparables: Robby Thompson, Tony Graffanino, Akinori Iwamura

The Department of Statistical Quirks had such fun with the Khris Davis .247 streak that we figure it's time to find out just how esoteric a fact can be and remain entertaining.

Warning: it's about fielding percentage. Are you ready? Hernández repeated his .981 fielding percentage at second base for the *fifth* consecutive year, a feat never before accomplished by any qualified position player. Should we make a t-shirt to celebrate the occasion? All right, fine, .981 24/7 doesn't quite have the same ring to it.

Still, is the consistency more fun because it belongs to Hernández, a player frequently called out for his miscues? Do the ongoing baserunning errors (Hernández led the league in outs on the bases) make it even more implausible that he owns a record of this nature? Is it fun because it's actually surprising that in thousands upon thousands of position player seasons, this has never happened before?

The true test of whether this fact is fun will come next fall, when we either feel the impulse to check Hernández's fielding percentage, or we don't. Then, and only then, we'll have our answer.

YEAR	TEAM	LVL	AGE	PA	DRC+	BABIP	BRR	FRAA	WARP
2018	PHI	MLB	28	708	101	.315	2.0	2B(154): 3.7	2.9
2019	PHI	MLB	29	667	90	.313	-1.2	2B(157): -4.7	0.8
2020	CLE	MLB	30	261	92	.364	-0.3	2B(58): 5.3	1.1
2021 FS	CLE	MLB	31	600	104	.329	0.5	2B 0	2.2
2021 DC	CLE	MLB	31	577	104	.329	0.5	2B 0	2.1

Cesar Hernandez, continued

Batted Ball Distribution

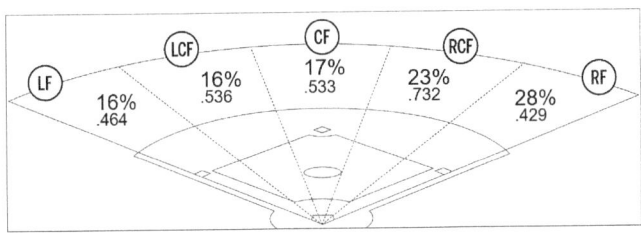

Strike Zone vs LHP

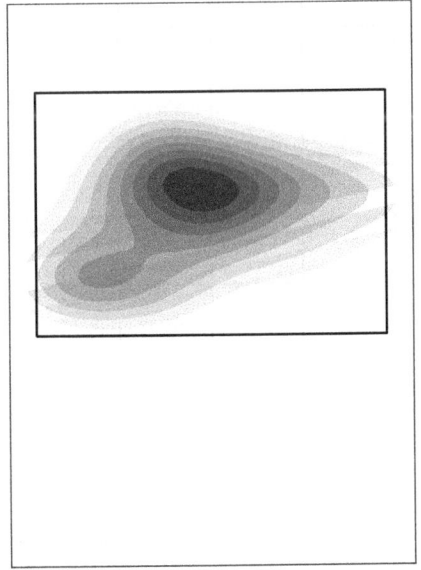

Strike Zone vs RHP

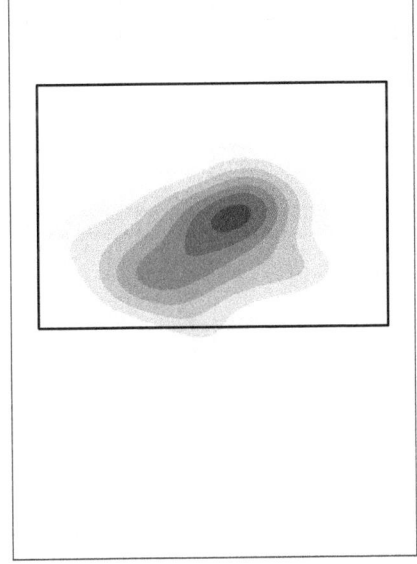

Jordan Luplow RF

Born: 09/26/93 Age: 27 Bats: R Throws: R
Height: 6'1" Weight: 195 Origin: Round 3, 2014 Draft (#100 overall)

YEAR	TEAM	LVL	AGE	PA	R	2B	3B	HR	RBI	BB	K	SB	CS	AVG/OBP/SLG
2018	IND	AAA	24	357	41	25	3	8	49	39	64	7	2	.287/.367/.462
2018	PIT	MLB	24	103	16	1	3	3	7	10	18	2	2	.185/.272/.359
2019	COL	AAA	25	57	12	3	0	2	7	10	14	2	1	.311/.456/.511
2019	CLE	MLB	25	261	42	15	1	15	38	33	61	3	2	.276/.372/.551
2020	CLE	MLB	26	92	8	5	1	2	8	12	19	0	1	.192/.304/.359
2021 FS	*CLE*	*MLB*	*27*	*600*	*76*	*26*	*2*	*26*	*77*	*64*	*140*	*2*	*2*	*.242/.334/.449*
2021 DC	*CLE*	*MLB*	*27*	*304*	*38*	*13*	*1*	*13*	*39*	*32*	*71*	*1*	*1*	*.242/.334/.449*

Comparables: Justin Upton, Dan Thomas, Brad Wilkerson

They say you can't predict baseball, but they probably weren't thinking about Luplow's platoon numbers when they said it, as he remains resolutely reliable in that facet of the game. Another year of solid performance against southpaws was undermined by his even more dependable inability to hit same-handed pitching. Luplow now owns the largest platoon split for a right-handed batter in major league history, with 393 points separating his damage against lefties from his failure against righties. (Pertinent fact: he is yet to record a hit against an offspeed pitch thrown by a righty in his major league career.) Despite that, Luplow defied probability and almost extended Cleveland's playoff run with a game-tying pinch-hit double against right-hander Jonathan Loaisiga. Maybe they were right after all.

YEAR	TEAM	LVL	AGE	PA	DRC+	BABIP	BRR	FRAA	WARP
2018	IND	AAA	24	357	140	.336	-1.7	LF(41): 4.3, RF(38): 1.4	2.3
2018	PIT	MLB	24	103	84	.197	-0.4	LF(16): 5.4, RF(11): -0.3, CF(3): 0.1	0.6
2019	COL	AAA	25	57	125	.414	-0.5	LF(10): 1.5, RF(2): -0.2	0.4
2019	CLE	MLB	25	261	125	.313	0.3	RF(42): 3.4, LF(34): 0.3, CF(4): -0.0	1.9
2020	CLE	MLB	26	92	97	.224	0.5	LF(21): -1.8, RF(9): 0.3	0.1
2021 FS	*CLE*	*MLB*	*27*	*600*	*113*	*.283*	*-0.5*	*RF 3, LF 1*	*2.8*
2021 DC	*CLE*	*MLB*	*27*	*304*	*113*	*.283*	*-0.3*	*RF 2, LF 0*	*1.3*

Jordan Luplow, continued

Batted Ball Distribution

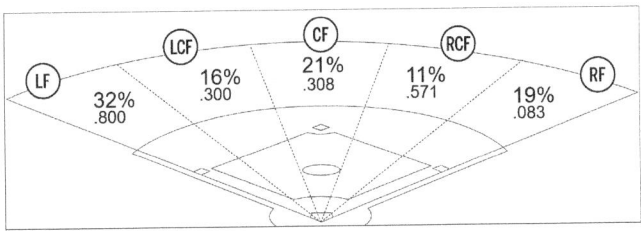

Strike Zone vs LHP

Strike Zone vs RHP

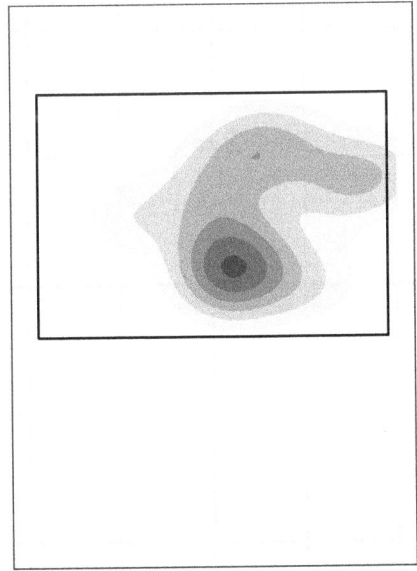
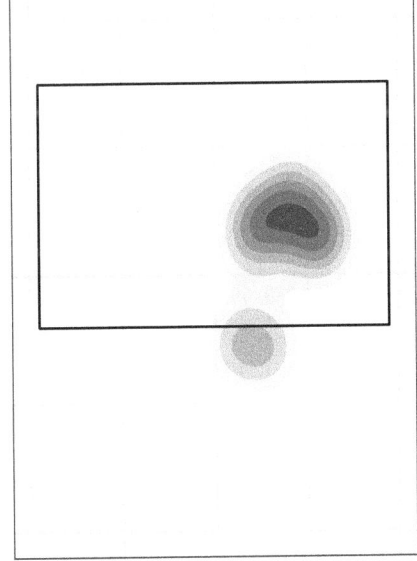

Cleveland 2021

Roberto Pérez C
Born: 12/23/88 Age: 32 Bats: R Throws: R
Height: 5'11" Weight: 220 Origin: Round 33, 2008 Draft (#1011 overall)

YEAR	TEAM	LVL	AGE	PA	R	2B	3B	HR	RBI	BB	K	SB	CS	AVG/OBP/SLG
2018	CLE	MLB	29	210	16	9	1	2	19	21	70	1	0	.168/.256/.263
2019	CLE	MLB	30	449	46	9	1	24	63	45	127	0	0	.239/.321/.452
2020	CLE	MLB	31	110	6	2	0	1	5	11	38	0	0	.165/.264/.216
2021 FS	CLE	MLB	32	600	66	17	1	18	59	69	197	1	1	.190/.290/.333
2021 DC	CLE	MLB	32	316	34	9	0	9	31	36	104	0	1	.190/.290/.333

Comparables: Todd Pratt, Kelly Stinnett, Jason Castro

YEAR	TEAM	P. COUNT	FRM RUNS	BLK RUNS	THRW RUNS	TOT RUNS
2018	CLE	7976	10.9	1.6	-0.2	12.2
2019	CLE	16305	15.5	8.8	1.5	25.8
2020	CLE	4053	1.3	0.5	-0.3	1.4
2021	CLE	12025	11.9	2.4	1.5	15.8
2021	CLE	12025	11.9	1.4	1.5	14.8

There was little opportunity for Pérez to prove that his unexpected offensive breakout was more than a one-year fluke. He suffered a strained shoulder in his first game, necessitating an IL stint, and he never recovered at the plate thereafter. The distinct similarity to Pérez's pre-breakout line (minus a home run or two) further confounds the matter. Fortunately, offensive production is not what he's paid for. Management validated as much by picking up his $5.5 million option on the strength of his defensive prowess, which earned him a second Gold Glove Award in a row. It would be a useful bonus for Cleveland if Pérez returned to slugging 20-plus homers, but they seem likely to remain devoted to him based on what he does behind the plate rather than at it.

YEAR	TEAM	LVL	AGE	PA	DRC+	BABIP	BRR	FRAA	WARP
2018	CLE	MLB	29	210	52	.257	-0.2	C(58): 11.1	0.9
2019	CLE	MLB	30	449	100	.285	-1.1	C(118): 25.7	4.7
2020	CLE	MLB	31	110	57	.259	-0.7	C(32): -0.3	-0.1
2021 FS	CLE	MLB	32	600	73	.264	-0.7	C 22	2.6
2021 DC	CLE	MLB	32	316	73	.264	-0.4	C 16	1.8

Roberto Pérez, continued

Batted Ball Distribution

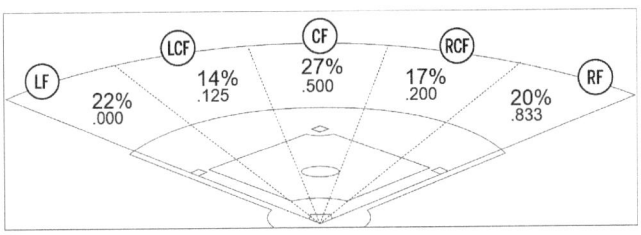

Strike Zone vs LHP   Strike Zone vs RHP

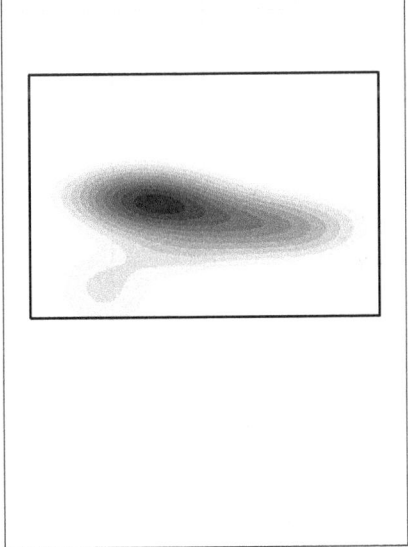

José Ramírez 3B

Born: 09/17/92 Age: 28 Bats: S Throws: R
Height: 5'9" Weight: 190 Origin: International Free Agent, 2009

YEAR	TEAM	LVL	AGE	PA	R	2B	3B	HR	RBI	BB	K	SB	CS	AVG/OBP/SLG
2018	CLE	MLB	25	698	110	38	4	39	105	106	80	34	6	.270/.387/.552
2019	CLE	MLB	26	542	68	33	3	23	83	52	74	24	4	.255/.327/.479
2020	CLE	MLB	27	254	45	16	1	17	46	31	43	10	3	.292/.386/.607
2021 FS	CLE	MLB	28	600	94	33	2	30	89	66	93	21	6	.271/.359/.513
2021 DC	CLE	MLB	28	642	101	35	2	32	95	71	99	22	7	.271/.359/.513

Comparables: Edgardo Alfonzo, Morgan Ensberg, Chipper Jones

You ought to know by now that Ramírez is an obsessed Mario Kart player. It's perhaps fair to write, then, that he succeeded in avoiding the banana peel that caused him to spin off course early in 2019. Instead, he followed up his second-half comeback by racing out of the blocks with a turbo-charged first week. Although Ramírez later fell back to the pack during the middle portion of the season, he shelled opposition pitchers at every turn down the stretch and bolted back to the top of the leaderboard to assert himself in the MVP race once more. Defensive metrics were divided over whether or not he bombed in the field, but he remains a star in the box.

YEAR	TEAM	LVL	AGE	PA	DRC+	BABIP	BRR	FRAA	WARP
2018	CLE	MLB	25	698	146	.252	5.2	3B(137): -3.5, 2B(16): -0.7	6.6
2019	CLE	MLB	26	542	115	.256	2.6	3B(126): 2.4	3.6
2020	CLE	MLB	27	254	146	.294	0.8	3B(57): -10.8	1.1
2021 FS	CLE	MLB	28	600	134	.281	1.2	3B -3, 2B 0	3.7
2021 DC	CLE	MLB	28	642	134	.281	1.3	3B -3	3.9

José Ramírez, continued

Batted Ball Distribution

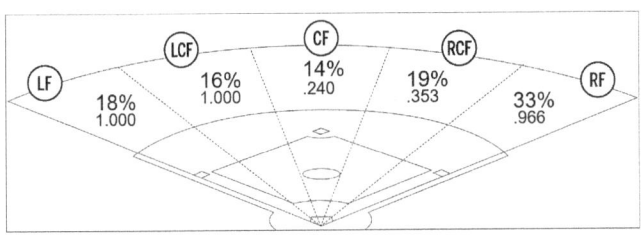

Strike Zone vs LHP

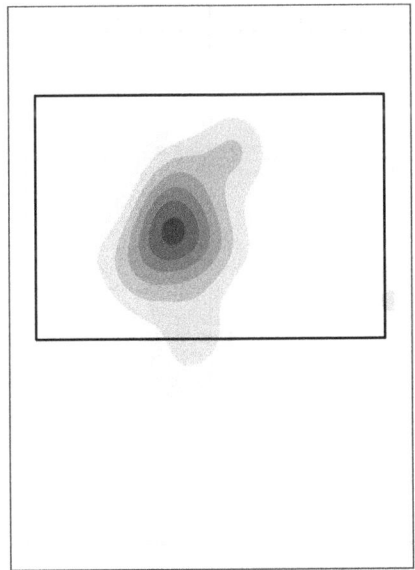

Strike Zone vs RHP

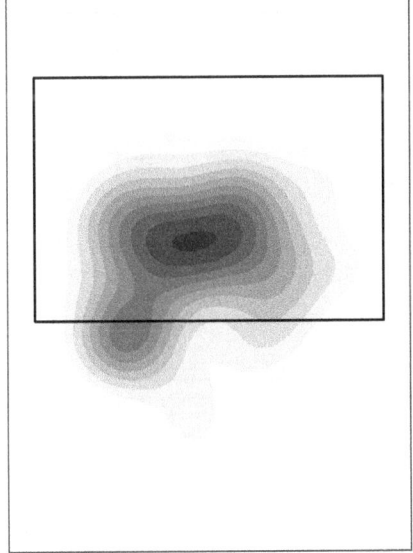

Cleveland 2021

Franmil Reyes   RF
Born: 07/07/95   Age: 26   Bats: R   Throws: R
Height: 6'5"   Weight: 265   Origin: International Free Agent, 2012

YEAR	TEAM	LVL	AGE	PA	R	2B	3B	HR	RBI	BB	K	SB	CS	AVG/OBP/SLG
2018	ELP	AAA	22	250	50	11	1	16	52	37	59	0	0	.324/.428/.614
2018	SD	MLB	22	285	36	9	0	16	31	24	80	0	0	.280/.340/.498
2019	CLE	MLB	23	194	26	10	0	10	35	18	63	0	0	.237/.304/.468
2019	SD	MLB	23	354	43	9	0	27	46	29	93	0	0	.255/.314/.536
2020	CLE	MLB	24	241	27	10	0	9	34	24	69	0	0	.275/.344/.450
2021 FS	CLE	MLB	25	600	83	26	1	32	89	56	175	0	0	.257/.331/.489
2021 DC	CLE	MLB	25	588	81	26	1	31	87	55	171	0	0	.257/.331/.489

Comparables: Wily Mo Pena, Jay Buhner, Victor Diaz

Reyes atoned for a slow start with a beastly August. When he started September by collecting eight hits in two games, his seasonal OPS stood at .962. That was as good as it got. Reyes did not hit another home run until the season's final day, at which point his numbers were almost identical to the year prior. The most consistent elements of his game at this point are the absurdity of his home runs, often mammoth in nature, and of his defense—remember, he's a full-time DH for a reason. If or until Reyes can overcome his streakiness, he's going to remain a frustrating talent who seems capable of much more than what shows up under his WAR column.

YEAR	TEAM	LVL	AGE	PA	DRC+	BABIP	BRR	FRAA	WARP
2018	ELP	AAA	22	250	165	.382	1.9	RF(46): -2.2	2.0
2018	SD	MLB	22	285	111	.345	0.3	RF(75): -7.1	0.3
2019	CLE	MLB	23	194	105	.301	-0.8	RF(3): 0.6	0.4
2019	SD	MLB	23	354	114	.268	0.4	RF(83): 1.4	1.6
2020	CLE	MLB	24	241	97	.355	0.0	LF(1): -0.1	0.4
2021 FS	CLE	MLB	25	600	118	.322	-1.0	LF 0, RF 0	2.6
2021 DC	CLE	MLB	25	588	118	.322	-1.0		2.3

Franmil Reyes, continued

Batted Ball Distribution

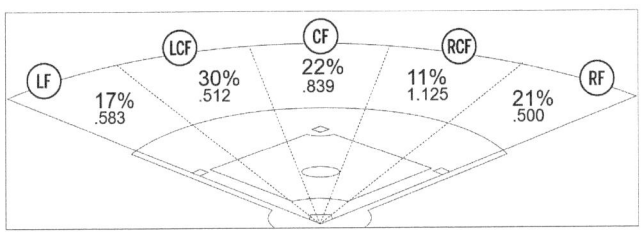

Strike Zone vs LHP

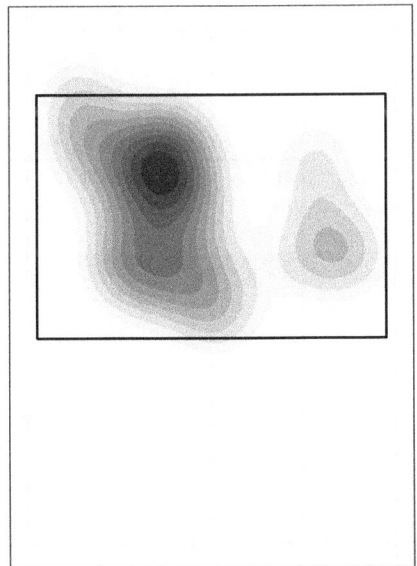

Strike Zone vs RHP

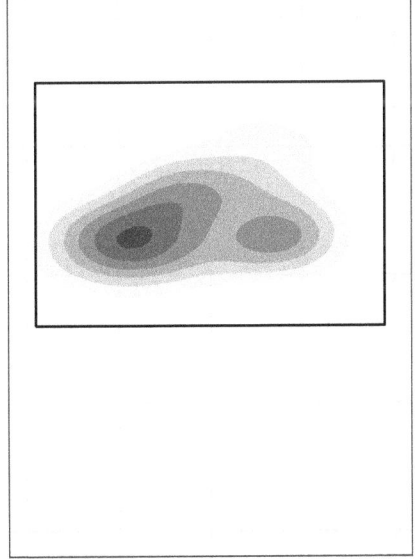

Amed Rosario SS

Born: 11/20/95 Age: 25 Bats: R Throws: R
Height: 6'2" Weight: 190 Origin: International Free Agent, 2012

YEAR	TEAM	LVL	AGE	PA	R	2B	3B	HR	RBI	BB	K	SB	CS	AVG/OBP/SLG
2018	NYM	MLB	22	592	76	26	8	9	51	29	119	24	11	.256/.295/.381
2019	NYM	MLB	23	655	75	30	7	15	72	31	124	19	10	.287/.323/.432
2020	NYM	MLB	24	147	20	3	1	4	15	4	34	0	1	.252/.272/.371
2021 FS	CLE	MLB	25	600	69	26	5	13	63	30	141	14	6	.259/.303/.399
2021 DC	CLE	MLB	25	459	53	20	4	10	48	23	108	10	5	.259/.303/.399

Comparables: Josh Rutledge, Ian Desmond, Michael Young

With Andrés Giménez looming on the horizon, the abridged 2020 season may have been Rosario's last chance to establish himself as a first-division starting shortstop. Despite a promising 2019 campaign as a 23-year-old, Rosario's 2020 accentuated his flaws and masked his strengths over a disappointing two months. His overaggressiveness at the plate was even more pronounced, as no player in the National League took a free pass less frequently. Oft credited for his athleticism, Rosario only attempted to steal a single base all season (he was thrown out) and his defense at shortstop continued to leave much to be desired. For years, a move to center field has been bandied about, and with this performance behind him, it might not be a bad idea to pick up a few more positions: a super-utility profile might be the new ceiling for this former top-10 prospect. Whethere he takes the field on the dirt or in the grass will be up to new management after Rosario was included in the four-player package that saw Francisco Lindor and Carlos Carrasco head to New York.

YEAR	TEAM	LVL	AGE	PA	DRC+	BABIP	BRR	FRAA	WARP
2018	NYM	MLB	22	592	82	.310	2.8	SS(146): -6.6	1.0
2019	NYM	MLB	23	655	95	.338	1.5	SS(152): -6.0, LF(1): -0.1	2.3
2020	NYM	MLB	24	147	68	.305	0.1	SS(44): -5.8	-0.8
2021 FS	CLE	MLB	25	600	89	.325	1.3	SS -1, LF 0	1.0
2021 DC	CLE	MLB	25	459	89	.325	1.0	CF 0, SS -1	0.8

Amed Rosario, continued

Batted Ball Distribution

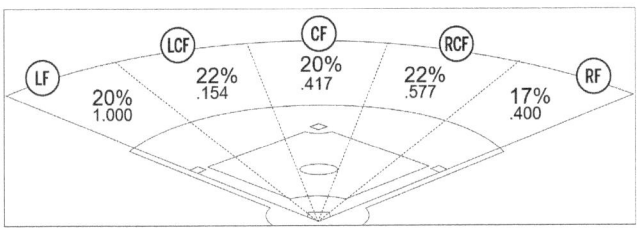

Strike Zone vs LHP

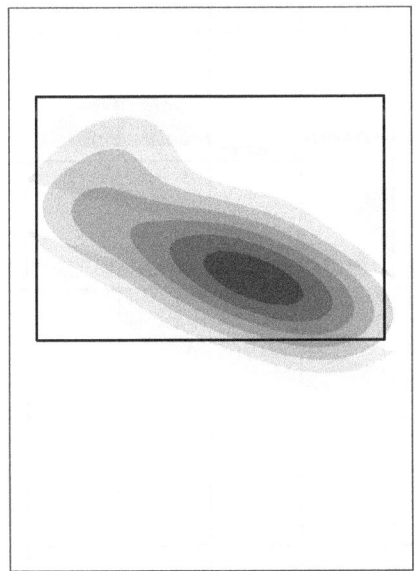

Strike Zone vs RHP

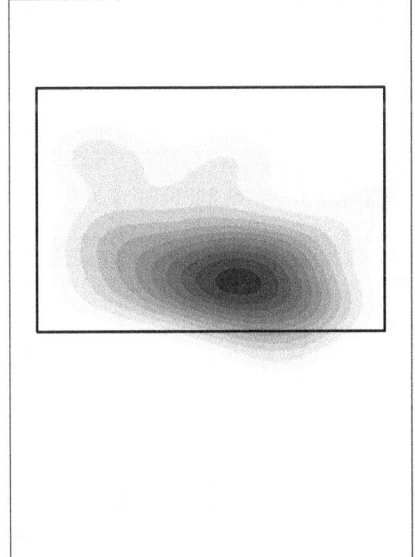

Eddie Rosario LF

Born: 09/28/91   Age: 29   Bats: L   Throws: R
Height: 6'1"   Weight: 180   Origin: Round 4, 2010 Draft (#135 overall)

YEAR	TEAM	LVL	AGE	PA	R	2B	3B	HR	RBI	BB	K	SB	CS	AVG/OBP/SLG
2018	MIN	MLB	26	592	87	31	2	24	77	30	104	8	2	.288/.323/.479
2019	MIN	MLB	27	590	91	28	1	32	109	22	86	3	1	.276/.300/.500
2020	MIN	MLB	28	231	31	7	0	13	42	19	34	3	1	.257/.316/.476
2021 FS	CLE	MLB	29	600	80	28	1	30	90	33	115	6	4	.271/.313/.485
2021 DC	CLE	MLB	29	562	75	26	1	28	84	31	108	6	3	.271/.313/.485

Comparables: Alfonso Soriano, Joe Carter, Mark Quinn

For those inclined to gin up a narrative based on two months of shaky data, Rosario's 2020 campaign provides sufficient fodder. Squint, and you'll note that his average exit velocity is squarely in line with career norms. From there, you can point to the best walk and strikeout numbers of his career and say that the only thing masking a mini-breakout was horrible luck on balls in play. Dig a little deeper though, and it's less clear whether he's actually changed anything about his approach. For one, he hasn't stopped offering at pitches off the plate: The uptick in his walk rate was actually the product of swinging far less often at pitches in the strike zone, which subsequently led to longer at-bats and more free passes. He also made more contact on every type of pitch, which is good when the ball is in the strike zone and generally lousy when it's not. If forced to choose whether Rosario is now a better hitter because he's become more selective, or simply coming off a strong two months against relatively weak pitching, the latter seems the likelier explanation.

YEAR	TEAM	LVL	AGE	PA	DRC+	BABIP	BRR	FRAA	WARP
2018	MIN	MLB	26	592	112	.316	6.8	LF(125): 5.9, RF(5): -0.2, CF(4): 0.1	3.6
2019	MIN	MLB	27	590	109	.273	0.9	LF(124): -8.8, RF(11): -0.5, CF(3): 0.0	1.5
2020	MIN	MLB	28	231	126	.248	0.9	LF(51): 0.1	1.4
2021 FS	CLE	MLB	29	600	111	.294	-0.1	LF 1, 3B 0	2.5
2021 DC	CLE	MLB	29	562	111	.294	-0.1	LF 1	2.3

Eddie Rosario, continued

Batted Ball Distribution

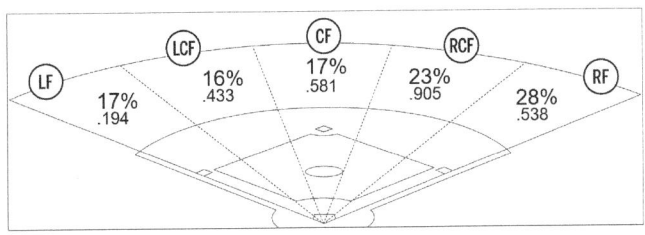

Strike Zone vs LHP   Strike Zone vs RHP

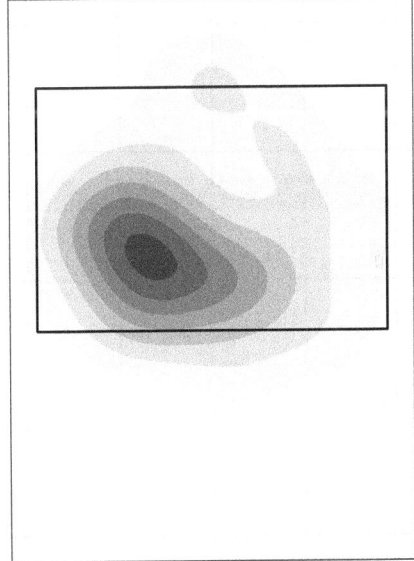

Shane Bieber RHP

Born: 05/31/95   Age: 26   Bats: R   Throws: R
Height: 6'3"   Weight: 200   Origin: Round 4, 2016 Draft (#122 overall)

YEAR	TEAM	LVL	AGE	W	L	SV	G	GS	IP	H	HR	BB/9	K/9	K	GB%	BABIP
2018	AKR	AA	23	3	0	0	5	5	31	26	1	0.3	8.7	30	47.3%	.278
2018	COL	AAA	23	3	1	0	8	8	48²	30	3	1.1	8.7	47	52.0%	.227
2018	CLE	MLB	23	11	5	0	20	19	114²	130	13	1.8	9.3	118	46.2%	.356
2019	CLE	MLB	24	15	8	0	34	33	214¹	186	31	1.7	10.9	259	44.4%	.298
2020	CLE	MLB	25	8	1	0	12	12	77¹	46	7	2.4	14.2	122	48.4%	.267
2021 FS	CLE	MLB	26	10	6	0	26	26	150	121	18	2.1	11.7	195	45.5%	.297
2021 DC	CLE	MLB	26	14	7	0	30	30	196.7	159	24	2.1	11.7	257	45.5%	.297

Comparables: Luis Severino, Danny Salazar, Joe Musgrove

The pitching Triple Crown; first in just about every other pitching category you can think of, and a few more besides; the third-best ERA+ of all time, and the best since Pedro Martinez's transcendent 2000 season; and so on. Bieber's accomplishments last year were diminished but not invalidated by the shortened season—only the very best hurlers can have 12-start runs this dominant. Bieber added a cutter to his already high-grade repertoire and ripped through every lineup he faced, striking out at least eight in each game and hitting double-digits in two-thirds of those starts. The one blemish on his record was a playoff stumble against the Yankees, a cruel end to an otherwise flawless season.

YEAR	TEAM	LVL	AGE	WHIP	ERA	DRA-	WARP	MPH	FB%	WHF	CSP
2018	AKR	AA	23	0.87	1.16	61	0.9				
2018	COL	AAA	23	0.74	1.66	69	1.2				
2018	CLE	MLB	23	1.33	4.55	74	2.6	94.7	57.4%	26.2%	
2019	CLE	MLB	24	1.05	3.28	75	4.9	94.4	45.8%	30.8%	
2020	CLE	MLB	25	0.87	1.63	53	2.6	95.3	53.6%	40.7%	
2021 FS	CLE	MLB	26	1.04	2.44	64	4.4	94.7	50.0%	33.2%	44.2%
2021 DC	CLE	MLB	26	1.04	2.44	64	5.8	94.7	50.0%	33.2%	44.2%

Shane Bieber, continued

Pitch Shape vs LHH

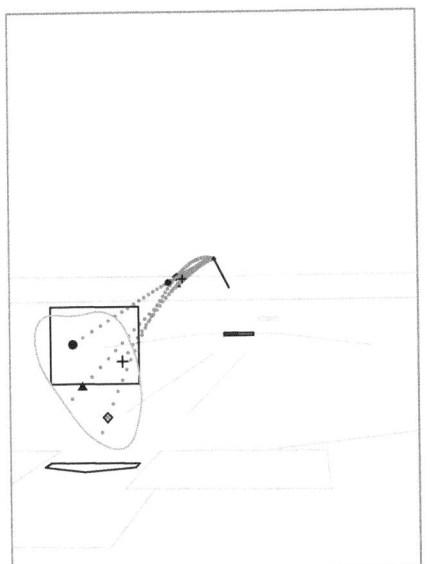

Pitch Shape vs RHH

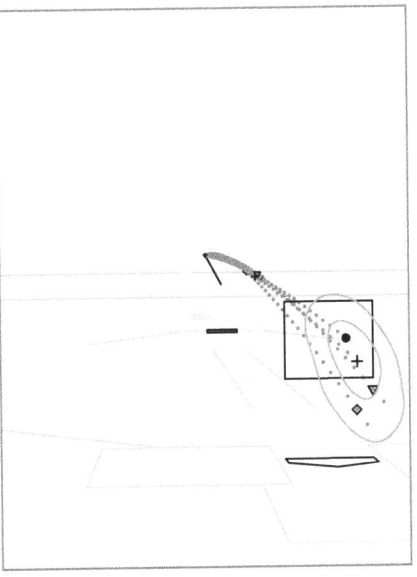

Type	Frequency	Velocity	H Movement	V Movement
● Fastball	37.4%	94.3 [105]	-8 [94]	-11.2 [111]
+ Cutter	16.2%	89.4 [107]	1.6 [98]	-22 [109]
▲ Changeup	8.5%	88.9 [115]	-14.2 [87]	-26.7 [102]
▽ Slider	11.6%	84.6 [103]	1.1 [84]	-37.3 [90]
◇ Curveball	26.3%	83.8 [120]	8 [102]	-48 [101]

Aaron Civale   RHP
Born: 06/12/95   Age: 26   Bats: R   Throws: R
Height: 6'2"   Weight: 215   Origin: Round 3, 2016 Draft (#92 overall)

YEAR	TEAM	LVL	AGE	W	L	SV	G	GS	IP	H	HR	BB/9	K/9	K	GB%	BABIP
2018	AKR	AA	23	5	7	0	21	21	106^1	115	12	1.8	6.6	78	46.5%	.310
2019	AKR	AA	24	4	0	0	5	5	30^1	26	3	1.8	7.1	24	42.2%	.264
2019	COL	AAA	24	3	1	0	8	8	42^1	38	4	1.9	9.8	46	37.8%	.298
2019	CLE	MLB	24	3	4	0	10	10	57^2	44	4	2.5	7.2	46	40.9%	.252
2020	CLE	MLB	25	4	6	0	12	12	74	82	11	1.9	8.4	69	45.1%	.333
2021 FS	CLE	MLB	26	9	8	0	26	26	150	144	21	2.7	8.0	133	42.9%	.290
2021 DC	CLE	MLB	26	10	8	0	27	27	159.7	153	23	2.7	8.0	142	42.9%	.290

Comparables: Tyler Duffey, Jakob Junis, Scott Lewis

A largely successful sophomore campaign unraveled for Civale in his last start of the season, and against the Pirates of all teams. A disastrous outing raised his ERA by almost a full run, washing away much of his progress. Civale increased his whiffs from his rookie season, and that could be credited to an increased reliance on his curveball. Alas, even with six pitches to choose from, he doesn't have a killer putaway offering. Cleveland has worked its magic with Shane Bieber and Zach Plesac, so it would be simultaneously remarkable and unsurprising if Civale became the latest in this rotation to vastly exceed expectations.

YEAR	TEAM	LVL	AGE	WHIP	ERA	DRA-	WARP	MPH	FB%	WHF	CSP
2018	AKR	AA	23	1.28	3.89	79	2.0				
2019	AKR	AA	24	1.05	2.67	100	0.0				
2019	COL	AAA	24	1.11	2.13	61	1.5				
2019	CLE	MLB	24	1.04	2.34	105	0.4	94.1	67.3%	21.4%	
2020	CLE	MLB	25	1.32	4.74	95	0.9	93.0	60.0%	25.0%	
2021 FS	CLE	MLB	26	1.26	3.76	92	2.1	93.4	62.4%	23.9%	44.1%
2021 DC	CLE	MLB	26	1.26	3.76	92	2.3	93.4	62.4%	23.9%	44.1%

Aaron Civale, continued

Pitch Shape vs LHH

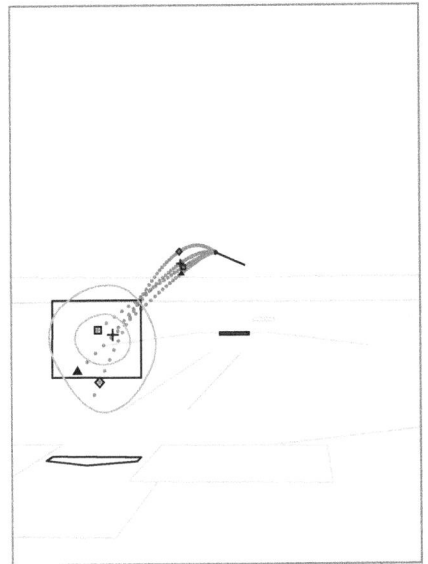

Pitch Shape vs RHH

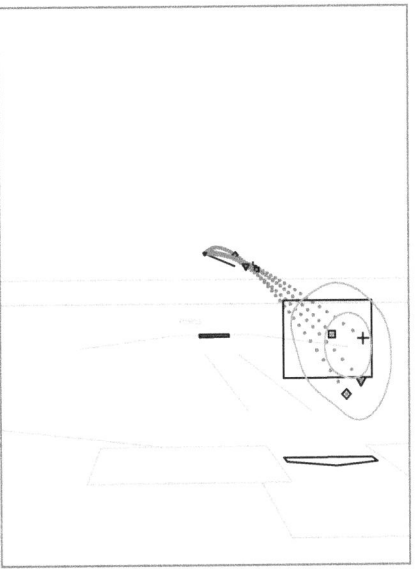

Type	Frequency	Velocity	H Movement	V Movement
☐ Sinker	29.2%	91.9 [97]	-12.2 [106]	-18.4 [107]
+ Cutter	28.6%	87.6 [95]	4.4 [116]	-23.6 [102]
▲ Changeup	9.2%	85.5 [101]	-13.8 [89]	-25.6 [105]
▽ Slider	9.7%	82.5 [93]	6.6 [105]	-37.2 [90]
◇ Curveball	21.1%	75.8 [89]	10.8 [113]	-57.5 [80]

Heath Hembree RHP

Born: 01/13/89 Age: 32 Bats: R Throws: R
Height: 6'4" Weight: 220 Origin: Round 5, 2010 Draft (#168 overall)

YEAR	TEAM	LVL	AGE	W	L	SV	G	GS	IP	H	HR	BB/9	K/9	K	GB%	BABIP
2018	BOS	MLB	29	4	1	0	67	0	60	53	10	4.0	11.4	76	39.7%	.295
2019	BOS	MLB	30	1	0	2	45	0	39^2	34	7	4.1	10.4	46	23.6%	.273
2020	PHI	MLB	31	3	0	0	22	0	19	26	9	3.8	9.5	20	31.7%	.333
2021 FS	CLE	MLB	32	2	2	0	57	0	50	43	9	3.6	9.5	52	32.8%	.274

Comparables: Hunter Strickland, Fernando Abad, Jeremy Jeffress

The best thing to happen to Hembree in 2020 was being paired with Brandon Workman in his trade from Boston to Philadelphia, so that his inability to retire hitters was overshadowed by Workman's even greater passion for not doing so.

YEAR	TEAM	LVL	AGE	WHIP	ERA	DRA-	WARP	MPH	FB%	WHF	CSP
2018	BOS	MLB	29	1.33	4.20	86	0.7	96.5	55.0%	31.6%	
2019	BOS	MLB	30	1.31	3.86	134	-0.5	95.8	69.8%	27.5%	
2020	PHI	MLB	31	1.79	9.00	169	-0.5	95.7	57.6%	26.9%	
2021 FS	CLE	MLB	32	1.28	4.05	95	0.4	96.0	61.6%	28.6%	45.5%

Heath Hembree, continued

Pitch Shape vs LHH

Pitch Shape vs RHH

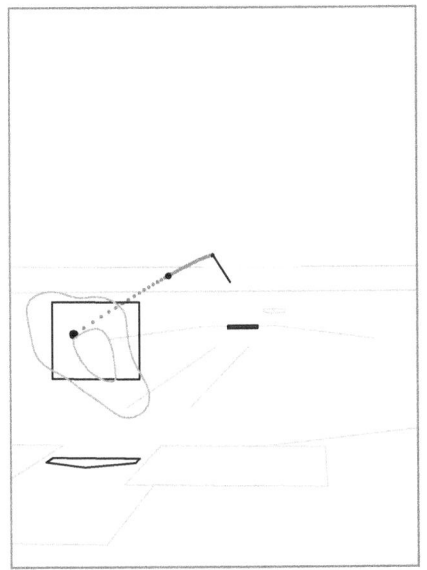
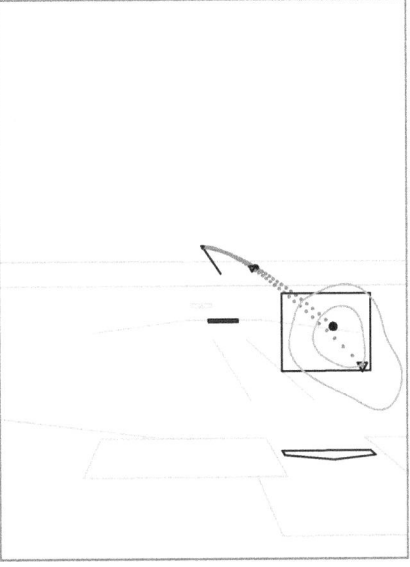

Type	Frequency	Velocity	H Movement	V Movement
● Fastball	57.6%	94.1 [105]	-9.4 [87]	-12.6 [107]
▽ Slider	32.8%	87.8 [117]	2.5 [90]	-25.8 [123]
◇ Curveball	9.6%	81.2 [110]	11.4 [115]	-45 [108]

Cam Hill RHP

Born: 05/24/94 Age: 27 Bats: R Throws: R
Height: 6'1" Weight: 200 Origin: Round 17, 2014 Draft (#518 overall)

YEAR	TEAM	LVL	AGE	W	L	SV	G	GS	IP	H	HR	BB/9	K/9	K	GB%	BABIP
2018	COL	AAA	24	0	0	3	16	0	13²	15	5	5.3	8.6	13	36.6%	.278
2019	LC	LO-A	25	0	0	0	5	0	6	3	0	1.5	12.0	8	35.7%	.214
2019	COL	AAA	25	4	2	1	21	0	24²	23	5	4.4	13.1	36	50.0%	.353
2020	CLE	MLB	26	2	0	1	18	0	18¹	11	4	2.5	7.9	16	38.8%	.156
2021 FS	CLE	MLB	27	2	2	0	57	0	50	45	8	3.6	9.3	51	39.7%	.286
2021 DC	CLE	MLB	27	2	2	0	53	0	57	51	9	3.6	9.3	59	39.7%	.286

Comparables: Jake Barrett, Trevor Gott, Dan Jennings

After a difficult six-year journey to the majors that included Tommy John surgery, Hill wasted no time in his debut by making a run at a major league record. His first five appearances were not only scoreless, Hill did not allow a walk or a hit, the second-longest such streak to start a career in major league history. He even notched his first career save in the process. Sadly, he fell one game short of tying Seranthony Domínguez when Yoán Moncada took him deep to start his sixth appearance. The numbers the rest of the way were far more pedestrian. Recapturing his pre-surgery velocity and developing better command will be key to finding more sustainable success. Regardless of what happens next, Hill had a debut to remember in a season no one will ever forget.

YEAR	TEAM	LVL	AGE	WHIP	ERA	DRA-	WARP	MPH	FB%	WHF	CSP
2018	COL	AAA	24	1.68	6.59	105	0.0				
2019	LC	LO-A	25	0.67	0.00	50	0.2				
2019	COL	AAA	25	1.42	4.74	79	0.6				
2020	CLE	MLB	26	0.87	4.91	114	0.0	93.5	48.5%	29.8%	
2021 FS	CLE	MLB	27	1.31	3.96	95	0.4	93.5	48.5%	29.8%	45.4%
2021 DC	CLE	MLB	27	1.31	3.96	95	0.4	93.5	48.5%	29.8%	45.4%

Cam Hill, continued

Pitch Shape vs LHH

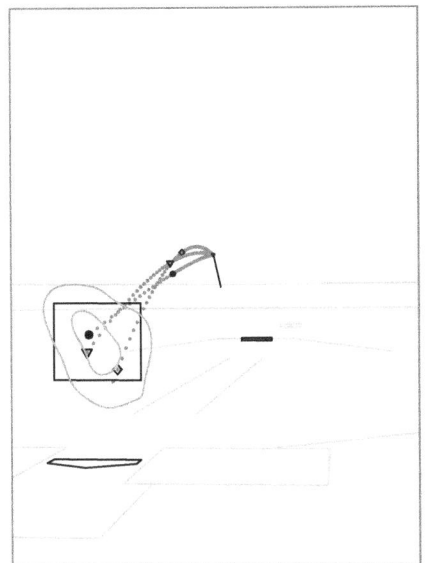

Pitch Shape vs RHH

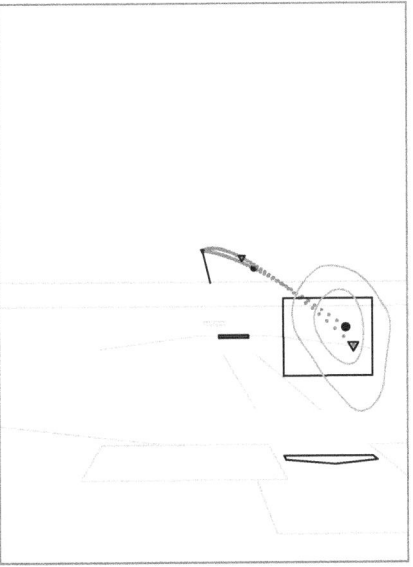

Type	Frequency	Velocity	H Movement	V Movement
● Fastball	47.8%	92.3 [99]	-3.5 [116]	-13.3 [105]
▽ Slider	35.3%	84 [100]	8.7 [113]	-33.4 [101]
◇ Curveball	15.6%	78.6 [100]	8.3 [103]	-56.4 [82]

Cleveland 2021

James Karinchak   RHP
Born: 09/22/95   Age: 25   Bats: R   Throws: R
Height: 6'3"   Weight: 215   Origin: Round 9, 2017 Draft (#282 overall)

YEAR	TEAM	LVL	AGE	W	L	SV	G	GS	IP	H	HR	BB/9	K/9	K	GB%	BABIP
2018	LC	LO-A	22	3	0	1	7	0	11^1	8	0	5.6	15.9	20	55.0%	.400
2018	LYN	HI-A	22	1	1	13	25	0	27	14	1	5.7	15.0	45	35.6%	.310
2018	AKR	AA	22	0	1	0	10	0	10^1	7	1	10.5	13.9	16	28.6%	.300
2019	INDB	ROK	23	0	0	0	3	0	3	0	0	6.0	24.0	8	0.0%	.000
2019	AKR	AA	23	0	0	6	10	0	10	2	0	1.8	21.6	24	55.6%	.222
2019	COL	AAA	23	1	1	2	17	0	17^1	14	2	6.8	21.8	42	47.8%	.571
2019	CLE	MLB	23	0	0	0	5	0	5^1	3	0	1.7	13.5	8	38.5%	.231
2020	CLE	MLB	24	1	2	1	27	0	27	14	1	5.3	17.7	53	22.5%	.342
2021 FS	CLE	MLB	25	3	2	29	57	0	50	34	6	5.1	15.6	86	35.2%	.318
2021 DC	CLE	MLB	25	2	2	29	53	0	57	39	7	5.1	15.6	98	35.2%	.318

Comparables: Roberto Osuna, Cody Allen, Trey Wingenter

Karinchak bristles with barely contained energy. His left foot taps the mound as though he's revving up for his leg kick. When he's particularly amped, his whole body rocks from side to side pre-pitch. He sprints off the field at the end of an inning, suggesting the act of pitching has rejuvenated rather than tired him. In some ways, it's reminiscent of Hunter Pence at the plate. Whereas Pence is quirky, however, Karinchak is altogether more threatening. Perhaps it's the way the ball explodes out of his hand, or the endless attempts his shoulders make to burst out of his jersey. Whatever the reason, it's working on hitters: almost half of whom fell to strikes.

YEAR	TEAM	LVL	AGE	WHIP	ERA	DRA-	WARP	MPH	FB%	WHF	CSP
2018	LC	LO-A	22	1.32	0.79	64	0.3				
2018	LYN	HI-A	22	1.15	1.00	60	0.7				
2018	AKR	AA	22	1.84	2.61	117	-0.1				
2019	INDB	ROK	23	0.67	0.00						
2019	AKR	AA	23	0.40	0.00	37	0.3				
2019	COL	AAA	23	1.56	4.67	43	0.7				
2019	CLE	MLB	23	0.75	1.69	79	0.1	97.6	56.4%	34.7%	
2020	CLE	MLB	24	1.11	2.67	62	0.8	96.8	50.2%	45.5%	
2021 FS	CLE	MLB	25	1.26	3.10	75	0.9	96.9	50.9%	44.2%	42.5%
2021 DC	CLE	MLB	25	1.26	3.10	75	1.1	96.9	50.9%	44.2%	42.5%

James Karinchak, continued

Pitch Shape vs LHH

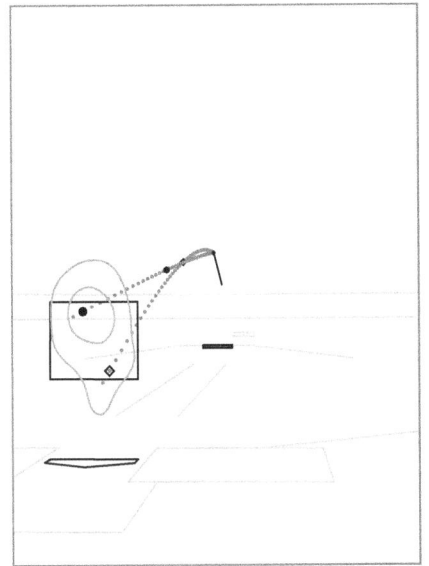

Pitch Shape vs RHH

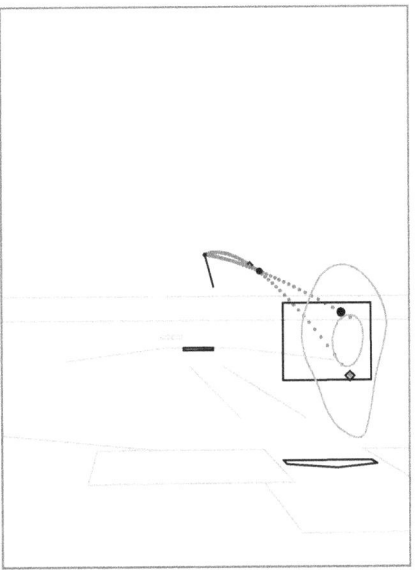

Type	Frequency	Velocity	H Movement	V Movement
● Fastball	49.8%	95.6 [110]	-4.6 [110]	-8.5 [119]
◇ Curveball	49.4%	83.3 [118]	-2.2 [60]	-41.5 [115]

Phil Maton RHP

Born: 03/25/93 Age: 28 Bats: R Throws: R
Height: 6'2" Weight: 206 Origin: Round 20, 2015 Draft (#597 overall)

YEAR	TEAM	LVL	AGE	W	L	SV	G	GS	IP	H	HR	BB/9	K/9	K	GB%	BABIP
2018	SA	AA	25	0	0	0	5	0	5²	5	1	1.6	11.1	7	33.3%	.286
2018	ELP	AAA	25	0	0	2	6	0	6¹	5	0	1.4	14.2	10	40.0%	.333
2018	SD	MLB	25	0	2	0	45	0	47¹	50	3	4.4	10.5	55	35.1%	.364
2019	ELP	AAA	26	2	1	2	13	0	18²	17	2	2.9	14.5	30	57.5%	.405
2019	COL	AAA	26	0	1	3	9	0	10²	5	1	3.4	14.3	17	44.4%	.235
2019	SD	MLB	26	0	0	0	21	0	24¹	34	6	2.2	7.4	20	44.3%	.350
2019	CLE	MLB	26	0	0	0	9	0	12¹	4	1	4.4	9.5	13	46.4%	.111
2020	CLE	MLB	27	3	3	0	23	0	21²	23	1	2.5	13.3	32	44.4%	.415
2021 FS	CLE	MLB	28	3	2	0	57	0	50	41	5	3.0	11.2	62	42.9%	.297
2021 DC	CLE	MLB	28	2	2	0	53	0	57	47	6	3.0	11.2	70	42.9%	.297

Comparables: Jonathan Holder, Fernando Cabrera, Dan Altavilla

Maton was a revelation for much of the season. His ultra high-spin four-seamer gained an edge with a velocity bump. While throwing 94 is unremarkable in the modern game, it proved lethal once combined with the fastball at the top of the zone, trademark knee-buckling curveball and further incorporation of a mid-80s cutter that also revolves at an incredible rate. Maton was thus one of the best relievers in the game by almost all measures, except for the one that counts: run prevention. Much of Maton's misfortune on balls in play came when he had runners on base, allowing almost 40 percent of those runners to score in a few bad outings and leaving his ERA looking much like his career mark. Sustaining this level of performance over a full season will produce results more representative of his dizzying stuff.

YEAR	TEAM	LVL	AGE	WHIP	ERA	DRA-	WARP	MPH	FB%	WHF	CSP
2018	SA	AA	25	1.06	1.59	28	0.2				
2018	ELP	AAA	25	0.95	2.84	56	0.2				
2018	SD	MLB	25	1.54	4.37	98	0.3	92.8	63.5%	32.7%	
2019	ELP	AAA	26	1.23	2.89	37	0.8				
2019	COL	AAA	26	0.84	2.53	39	0.4				
2019	SD	MLB	26	1.64	7.77	116	-0.1	93.3	77.1%	24.8%	
2019	CLE	MLB	26	0.81	2.92	55	0.4	92.5	70.4%	24.7%	
2020	CLE	MLB	27	1.34	4.57	70	0.5	95.1	79.7%	37.3%	
2021 FS	CLE	MLB	28	1.16	2.96	75	0.9	93.7	73.7%	31.3%	47.2%
2021 DC	CLE	MLB	28	1.16	2.96	75	1.1	93.7	73.7%	31.3%	47.2%

Phil Maton, continued

Pitch Shape vs LHH

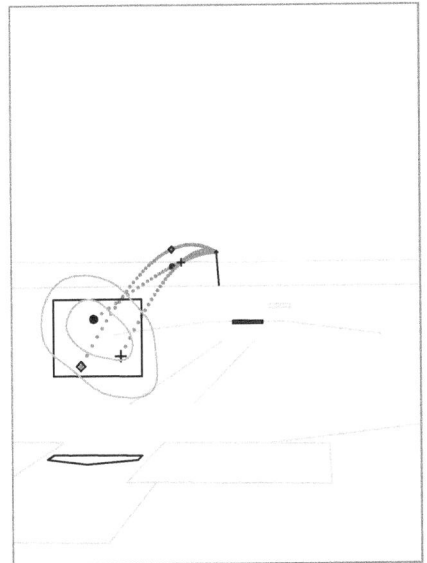

Pitch Shape vs RHH

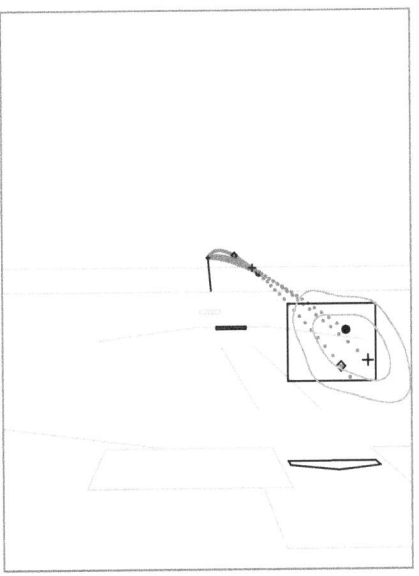

Type	Frequency	Velocity	H Movement	V Movement
● Fastball	46.7%	93.7 [104]	-0.5 [130]	-15.7 [99]
+ Cutter	31.5%	85.5 [82]	9.2 [147]	-34.3 [61]
◇ Curveball	20.2%	76.9 [93]	16.1 [134]	-51.9 [92]

Triston McKenzie RHP

Born: 08/02/97 Age: 23 Bats: R Throws: R
Height: 6'5" Weight: 165 Origin: Round 1, 2015 Draft (#42 overall)

YEAR	TEAM	LVL	AGE	W	L	SV	G	GS	IP	H	HR	BB/9	K/9	K	GB%	BABIP
2018	AKR	AA	20	7	4	0	16	16	90^2	63	8	2.8	8.6	87	33.3%	.234
2020	CLE	MLB	22	2	1	0	8	6	33^1	21	6	2.4	11.3	42	40.0%	.217
2021 FS	CLE	MLB	23	10	7	0	26	26	150	133	24	2.8	10.2	169	36.2%	.289
2021 DC	CLE	MLB	23	7	6	0	22	22	111	98	18	2.8	10.2	125	36.2%	.289

Comparables: Noah Syndergaard, Tyler Skaggs, Jenrry Mejia

McKenzie overwhelmed hitters at times during his rookie season. He punched out 10 in his debut, and he limited opponents to three hits or fewer in each of his first five turns. The durability concerns that have plagued his career resurfaced alarmingly quickly: he went from sitting at 95 mph in his first start to 91 in his sixth, at which point he was moved to the bullpen in preparation for the playoffs. McKenzie still looks like a strong gust of wind could topple him from the mound and, while he has a starter's arsenal, his failure to maintain velocity over even half of a shortened season renews the doubts about his ability to do so over 30-plus starts.

YEAR	TEAM	LVL	AGE	WHIP	ERA	DRA-	WARP	MPH	FB%	WHF	CSP
2018	AKR	AA	20	1.00	2.68	86	1.4				
2020	CLE	MLB	22	0.90	3.24	85	0.6	95.3	53.3%	29.2%	
2021 FS	CLE	MLB	23	1.20	3.56	87	2.5	95.3	53.3%	29.2%	45.6%
2021 DC	CLE	MLB	23	1.20	3.56	87	1.8	95.3	53.3%	29.2%	45.6%

Triston McKenzie, continued

Pitch Shape vs LHH

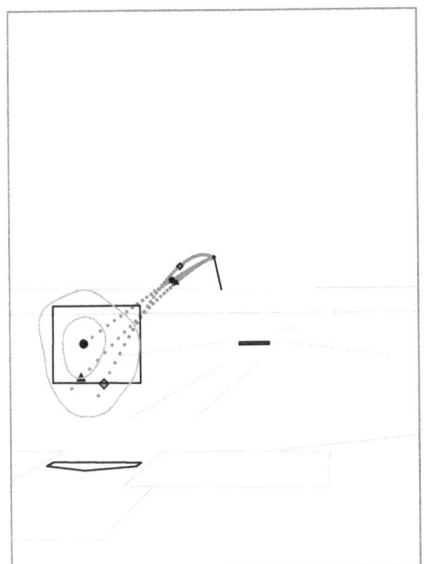

Pitch Shape vs RHH

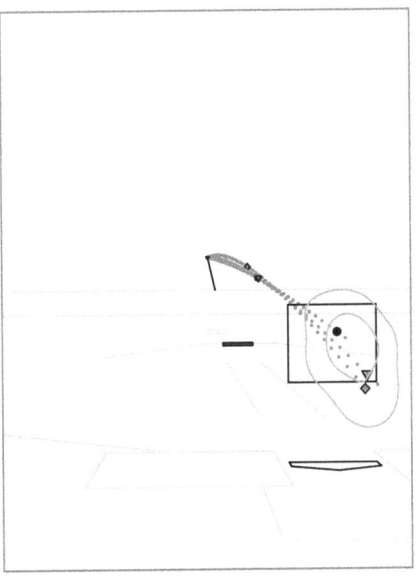

Type	Frequency	Velocity	H Movement	V Movement
● Fastball	53.3%	92.9 [101]	-3.9 [114]	-10.5 [113]
▲ Changeup	10.0%	86.9 [107]	-8.4 [118]	-22.3 [114]
▽ Slider	20.2%	86.5 [111]	2.4 [89]	-28 [117]
◇ Curveball	16.5%	80.2 [106]	5.8 [93]	-43.4 [111]

Blake Parker RHP

Born: 06/19/85   Age: 36   Bats: R   Throws: R
Height: 6'3"   Weight: 225   Origin: Round 16, 2006 Draft (#479 overall)

YEAR	TEAM	LVL	AGE	W	L	SV	G	GS	IP	H	HR	BB/9	K/9	K	GB%	BABIP
2018	LAA	MLB	33	2	1	14	67	0	66^1	63	12	2.6	9.5	70	34.8%	.297
2019	PHI	MLB	34	2	1	0	23	2	25	19	6	2.2	11.2	31	28.3%	.250
2019	MIN	MLB	34	1	2	10	37	0	36^1	34	7	4.0	8.4	34	43.8%	.276
2020	PHI	MLB	35	3	0	0	14	1	16	12	2	5.1	14.1	25	37.1%	.303
2021 FS	CLE	MLB	36	2	2	0	57	0	50	43	7	3.7	10.2	56	38.6%	.283

Comparables: Shawn Kelley, Tyler Clippard, Mark Melancon

There was a moment in 2020 when Parker appeared to be on verge of completely liquefying on the mound. Fluid poured out of him, dripped off his fingertips and saturated his uniform, to the point that the cameras zoomed in to show anyone watching that a man was about to be soaked into the mound. Though moist, Parker made his splitter effective again for the month of August—fortunate, given that he went back to it a little more than in 2019. Parker was typically good for allowing a baserunner or two, but he set himself apart from the rest of the Phillies bullpen by allowing only a single unearned run in his first eight appearances. His formula of never throwing hittable pitches, striking out everyone he didn't walk, actually did the job. The rest of the year was a bit more of an adventure, with a couple of relief disasters that helped him blend right in, especially on nights he followed the walks with home runs. Still, opposing hitters could only touch him for a .200 BA, the best rate of his career, so whatever he was sweating out, he didn't miss.

YEAR	TEAM	LVL	AGE	WHIP	ERA	DRA-	WARP	MPH	FB%	WHF	CSP
2018	LAA	MLB	33	1.24	3.26	115	-0.2	94.0	58.1%	25.1%	
2019	PHI	MLB	34	1.00	5.04	60	0.7	92.0	47.9%	29.2%	
2019	MIN	MLB	34	1.38	4.21	108	0.0	92.9	55.5%	26.2%	
2020	PHI	MLB	35	1.31	2.81	76	0.3	92.0	41.3%	29.4%	
2021 FS	CLE	MLB	36	1.27	3.81	90	0.5	92.9	51.5%	27.2%	44.8%

Blake Parker, continued

Pitch Shape vs LHH

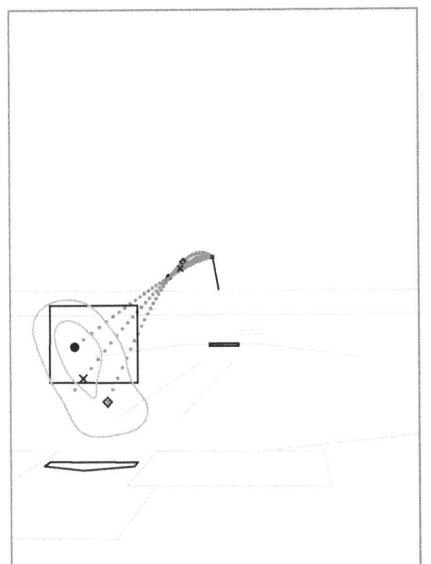

Pitch Shape vs RHH

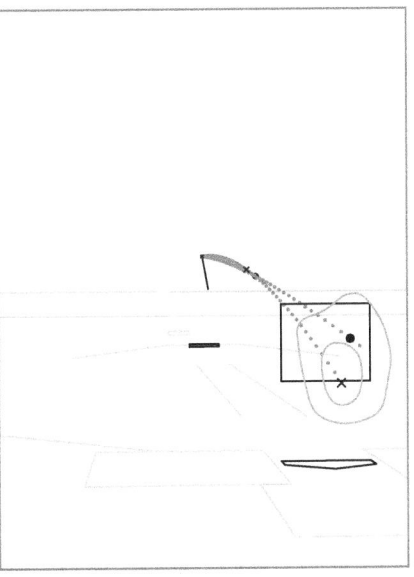

Type	Frequency	Velocity	H Movement	V Movement
● Fastball	40.5%	90.8 [94]	-2.6 [120]	-14.7 [101]
✕ Splitter	41.1%	80.2 [77]	-7.9 [100]	-37 [75]
◇ Curveball	16.5%	76.3 [91]	4.7 [88]	-52.1 [92]

Oliver Pérez   LHP

Born: 08/15/81   Age: 39   Bats: L   Throws: L
Height: 6'3"   Weight: 225   Origin: International Free Agent, 1999

YEAR	TEAM	LVL	AGE	W	L	SV	G	GS	IP	H	HR	BB/9	K/9	K	GB%	BABIP
2018	SWB	AAA	36	1	0	0	16	0	14	17	1	1.9	9.6	15	33.3%	.421
2018	CLE	MLB	36	1	1	0	51	0	32^1	17	1	1.9	12.0	43	45.6%	.239
2019	CLE	MLB	37	2	4	1	67	0	40^2	38	5	2.7	10.6	48	43.6%	.314
2020	CLE	MLB	38	1	1	1	21	0	18	13	0	3.0	7.0	14	44.9%	.265
2021 FS	CLE	MLB	39	2	2	0	57	0	50	45	6	3.0	9.4	52	41.4%	.292

Comparables: Arthur Rhodes, Tom Gordon, Rich Hill

Pérez led the American League in 2019 with 33 appearances facing two or fewer batters, which made him one of the obvious potential casualties of the three-batter minimum rule. It might have cost him his typical platoon advantage and a few strikeouts, but it had as little effect on his topline run prevention as it did on the length of games. He was called upon more sparingly than he would have been in the days of the LOOGY, and his peripherals suggest that a longer season might have eventually had a negative effect on those results. Then again, they would also have suggested that his career was unlikely to last much longer a decade ago, and he's now the longest-tenured pitcher in the Show, so there's no sense counting him out just yet.

YEAR	TEAM	LVL	AGE	WHIP	ERA	DRA-	WARP	MPH	FB%	WHF	CSP
2018	SWB	AAA	36	1.43	2.57	71	0.3				
2018	CLE	MLB	36	0.74	1.39	58	0.9	93.9	51.0%	35.2%	
2019	CLE	MLB	37	1.23	3.98	87	0.5	94.0	51.0%	28.3%	
2020	CLE	MLB	38	1.06	2.00	99	0.2	92.5	56.9%	19.4%	
2021 FS	CLE	MLB	39	1.23	3.64	88	0.6	93.5	52.9%	26.6%	52.3%

Oliver Pérez, continued

Pitch Shape vs LHH

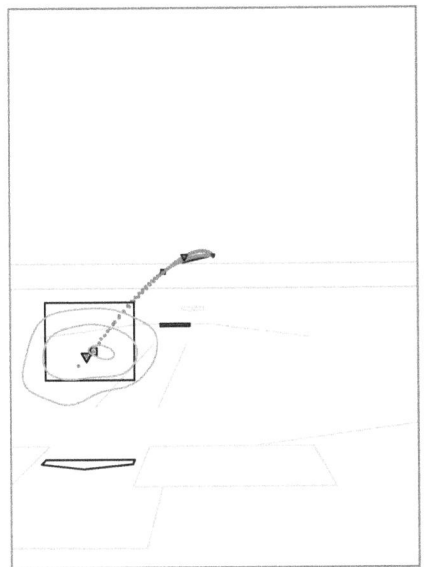

Pitch Shape vs RHH

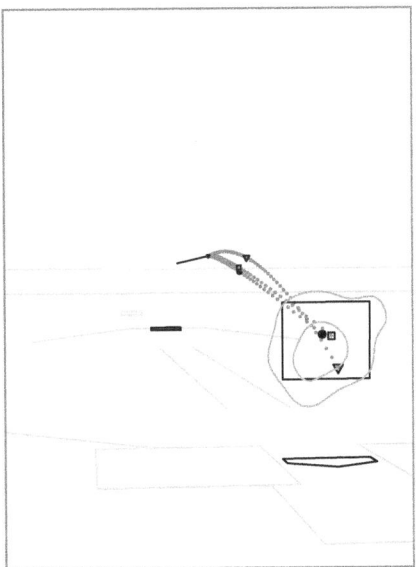

Type	Frequency	Velocity	H Movement	V Movement
● Fastball	13.3%	89.6 [91]	10.3 [83]	-16.6 [96]
□ Sinker	41.3%	90.1 [88]	15.8 [80]	-23.5 [90]
▽ Slider	41.3%	76.3 [66]	-9.1 [114]	-43.2 [73]

Cleveland Player Analysis - 53

Zach Plesac RHP

Born: 01/21/95 Age: 26 Bats: R Throws: R
Height: 6'3" Weight: 220 Origin: Round 12, 2016 Draft (#362 overall)

YEAR	TEAM	LVL	AGE	W	L	SV	G	GS	IP	H	HR	BB/9	K/9	K	GB%	BABIP
2018	LYN	HI-A	23	8	5	0	22	22	122²	124	8	2.4	8.1	111	42.7%	.330
2018	AKR	AA	23	3	1	0	4	4	22	19	1	1.6	8.6	21	27.9%	.305
2019	AKR	AA	24	1	1	0	6	6	37¹	23	0	1.4	8.2	34	48.5%	.237
2019	COL	AAA	24	3	1	0	4	4	26¹	19	2	1.0	10.6	31	27.7%	.270
2019	CLE	MLB	24	8	6	0	21	21	115²	102	19	3.1	6.8	88	39.2%	.257
2020	CLE	MLB	25	4	2	0	8	8	55¹	38	8	1.0	9.3	57	38.0%	.224
2021 FS	CLE	MLB	26	9	8	0	26	26	150	139	25	2.6	8.9	147	38.4%	.284
2021 DC	CLE	MLB	26	10	8	0	27	27	154	142	26	2.6	8.9	152	38.4%	.284

Comparables: Zach Eflin, Erick Fedde, Daniel Mengden

The story of Plesac's season was his violation of the COVID-19 protocols, an error that was compounded by a non-apology video that he filmed while driving without a seatbelt. (Clearly he has an abnormally and uncomfortably high tolerance for risk.) In said video, he defended his acts and blamed the fallout on negative media coverage—as opposed to, say, one of his teammates threatening to retire if he remained on the active roster. Predictably, the team demoted him and left him out of the rotation for more than three weeks, which is a long time when the season lasts two months. There are a lot of sad elements to Plesac's 2020; one of the saddest is that, if he had sacrificed his individual desires for the sake of the collective benefit, then this space would've been devoted to singing his praises after a seeming breakout.

YEAR	TEAM	LVL	AGE	WHIP	ERA	DRA-	WARP	MPH	FB%	WHF	CSP
2018	LYN	HI-A	23	1.28	4.04	81	2.2				
2018	AKR	AA	23	1.05	2.45	85	0.3				
2019	AKR	AA	24	0.78	0.96	53	1.1				
2019	COL	AAA	24	0.84	2.73	47	1.1				
2019	CLE	MLB	24	1.23	3.81	128	-0.6	95.4	50.6%	21.7%	
2020	CLE	MLB	25	0.80	2.28	89	0.8	94.4	37.6%	29.8%	
2021 FS	CLE	MLB	26	1.21	3.70	91	2.2	95.0	45.7%	24.8%	49.7%
2021 DC	CLE	MLB	26	1.21	3.70	91	2.3	95.0	45.7%	24.8%	49.7%

Zach Plesac, continued

Pitch Shape vs LHH

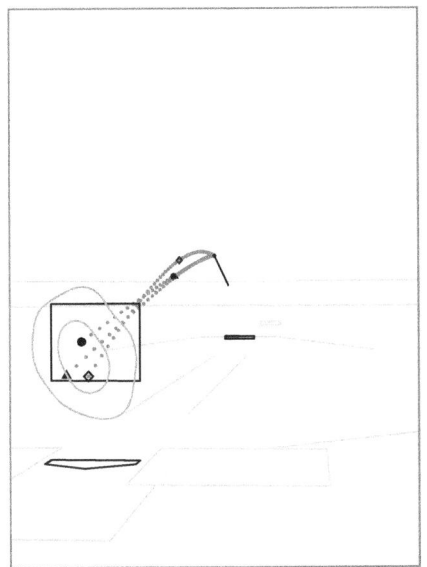

Pitch Shape vs RHH

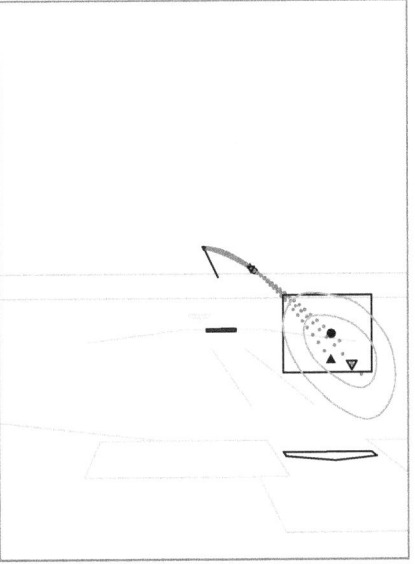

Type	Frequency	Velocity	H Movement	V Movement
● Fastball	37.6%	92.9 [101]	-6.8 [100]	-13.2 [106]
▲ Changeup	25.3%	86.2 [104]	-10.7 [105]	-24.3 [109]
▽ Slider	27.8%	86.4 [111]	1.5 [86]	-27.6 [118]
◇ Curveball	9.3%	79.3 [103]	1.6 [76]	-44 [110]

Cleveland 2021

Adam Plutko   RHP

Born: 10/03/91   Age: 29   Bats: R   Throws: R
Height: 6'3"   Weight: 215   Origin: Round 11, 2013 Draft (#321 overall)

YEAR	TEAM	LVL	AGE	W	L	SV	G	GS	IP	H	HR	BB/9	K/9	K	GB%	BABIP
2018	COL	AAA	26	7	3	0	14	14	84^2	47	5	1.7	8.6	81	27.2%	.199
2018	CLE	MLB	26	4	5	1	17	12	76^2	78	21	2.7	7.0	60	27.3%	.259
2019	COL	AAA	27	1	3	0	4	4	15^2	21	1	2.3	9.2	16	22.0%	.408
2019	CLE	MLB	27	7	5	0	21	20	109^1	115	22	2.1	6.4	78	31.6%	.280
2020	CLE	MLB	28	2	2	1	10	4	27^2	30	5	2.3	4.9	15	26.9%	.287
2021 FS	CLE	MLB	29	9	9	0	26	26	150	150	32	2.6	6.9	115	29.5%	.270
2021 DC	CLE	MLB	29	7	6	0	39	12	95.7	96	21	2.6	6.9	73	29.5%	.270

Comparables: Dylan Covey, Alec Mills, Austin Voth

Autocorrect insists on changing Plutko to Pluto, which serves as an unintentionally cutting yet apt evaluation of his place within Cleveland's pitching galaxy. He's always the last name on the leaderboards, orbiting a different plane than the one occupied by the Civales, let alone the Biebers and the Plesacs. Because he's out of options, and because he's never finished above the replacement-level line, it's possible that he loses his planetary status sooner than later, perhaps leaving him drifting into the deep space that is the waiver wire right around the season's launch date.

YEAR	TEAM	LVL	AGE	WHIP	ERA	DRA-	WARP	MPH	FB%	WHF	CSP
2018	COL	AAA	26	0.74	1.70	81	1.4				
2018	CLE	MLB	26	1.32	5.28	161	-1.7	92.8	59.8%	19.0%	
2019	COL	AAA	27	1.60	7.47	135	0.0				
2019	CLE	MLB	27	1.29	4.86	159	-2.4	92.5	54.0%	18.9%	
2020	CLE	MLB	28	1.34	4.88	168	-0.8	92.3	78.3%	23.3%	
2021 FS	CLE	MLB	29	1.29	4.50	107	0.8	92.5	60.5%	19.9%	46.4%
2021 DC	CLE	MLB	29	1.29	4.50	107	0.4	92.5	60.5%	19.9%	46.4%

Adam Plutko, continued

Pitch Shape vs LHH

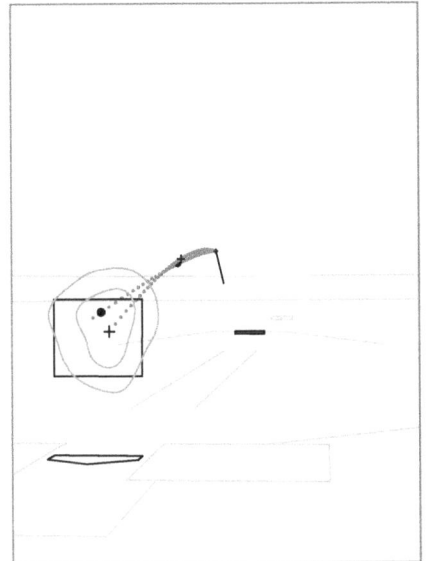

Pitch Shape vs RHH

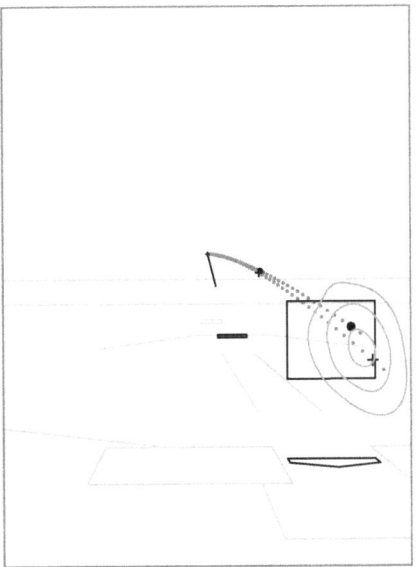

Type	Frequency	Velocity	H Movement	V Movement
● Fastball	50.2%	91.2 [96]	-3.8 [114]	-13.5 [105]
+ Cutter	28.0%	86.7 [90]	3.2 [109]	-24.7 [98]
▲ Changeup	4.5%	84.5 [97]	-8.2 [118]	-23.8 [110]
▽ Slider	4.9%	84.6 [103]	4.6 [98]	-30.4 [110]
◇ Curveball	12.3%	77 [94]	10 [110]	-50.6 [95]

Cal Quantrill RHP

Born: 02/10/95   Age: 26   Bats: L   Throws: R
Height: 6'3"   Weight: 195   Origin: Round 1, 2016 Draft (#8 overall)

YEAR	TEAM	LVL	AGE	W	L	SV	G	GS	IP	H	HR	BB/9	K/9	K	GB%	BABIP
2018	SA	AA	23	6	5	0	22	22	117	135	12	2.9	7.8	101	44.2%	.339
2018	ELP	AAA	23	3	1	0	6	6	31	39	4	1.5	6.4	22	48.6%	.337
2019	ELP	AAA	24	4	2	0	7	7	35^2	38	3	3.0	8.3	33	50.5%	.324
2019	SD	MLB	24	6	8	0	23	18	103	106	15	2.4	7.8	89	43.3%	.297
2020	CLE	MLB	25	2	0	1	18	3	32	31	4	2.2	8.7	31	44.6%	.310
2021 FS	CLE	MLB	26	9	8	0	26	26	150	145	21	3.0	8.1	134	44.2%	.292
2021 DC	CLE	MLB	26	6	5	0	34	12	76	73	10	3.0	8.1	68	44.2%	.292

Comparables: Trevor Williams, Kevin Gausman, Yonny Chirinos

Sometimes it pays to zig when everyone else is zagging. Quantrill doubled-down on a contrarian strategy in the modern game, betting on his sinker while fading his four-seam fastball. It appeared to pay off in the short term, bringing success more befitting of his original draft and prospect status, even as the Padres opted to swap him for a more well-established pitcher. Quantrill's sinker more closely resembles his changeup and slider at release, a similarity that depressed the quality of contact and enabled the right-hander to keep his four-seamer in reserve as a putaway option. There's no sense reading too much into a small sample, but we're interested to learn whether a winter under Cleveland's watch can help Quantrill take the next step forward, the way Bieber and Plesac have the past few years.

YEAR	TEAM	LVL	AGE	WHIP	ERA	DRA-	WARP	MPH	FB%	WHF	CSP
2018	SA	AA	23	1.48	5.15	84	1.6				
2018	ELP	AAA	23	1.42	3.48	85	0.5				
2019	ELP	AAA	24	1.40	4.54	77	1.0				
2019	SD	MLB	24	1.30	5.16	89	1.5	95.9	56.7%	22.4%	
2020	CLE	MLB	25	1.22	2.25	93	0.4	96.0	54.0%	25.0%	
2021 FS	CLE	MLB	26	1.30	3.90	94	1.9	95.9	55.9%	23.1%	45.6%
2021 DC	CLE	MLB	26	1.30	3.90	94	0.8	95.9	55.9%	23.1%	45.6%

Cal Quantrill, continued

Pitch Shape vs LHH

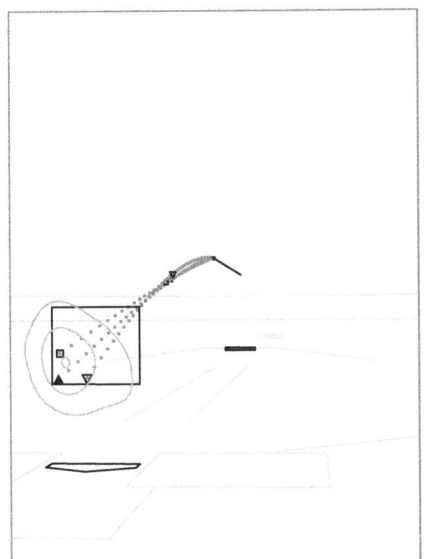

Pitch Shape vs RHH

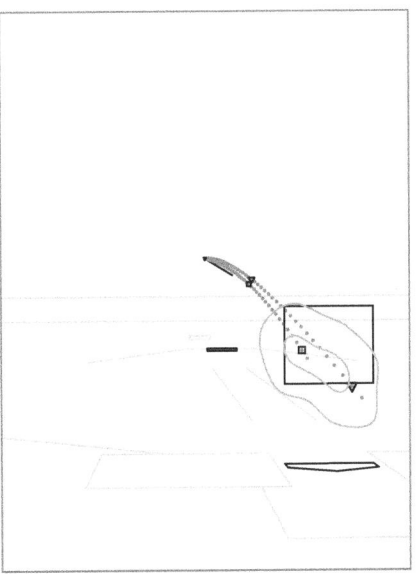

Type	Frequency	Velocity	H Movement	V Movement
● Fastball	7.1%	95.3 [109]	-7.5 [96]	-12.6 [107]
□ Sinker	46.6%	94.9 [113]	-11.2 [114]	-14.8 [119]
▲ Changeup	10.7%	85.6 [102]	-7.7 [122]	-24 [110]
▽ Slider	35.2%	86.2 [110]	2.9 [91]	-33.3 [101]

Nick Wittgren RHP

Born: 05/29/91 Age: 30 Bats: R Throws: R
Height: 6'2" Weight: 216 Origin: Round 9, 2012 Draft (#287 overall)

YEAR	TEAM	LVL	AGE	W	L	SV	G	GS	IP	H	HR	BB/9	K/9	K	GB%	BABIP
2018	NO	AAA	27	0	5	2	25	0	29^1	34	4	2.5	10.4	34	44.3%	.357
2018	MIA	MLB	27	2	1	0	32	0	33^2	29	1	4.0	8.3	31	45.5%	.283
2019	CLE	MLB	28	5	1	4	55	0	57^2	47	10	2.3	9.4	60	39.1%	.253
2020	CLE	MLB	29	2	0	0	25	0	23^2	18	4	2.3	10.6	28	32.2%	.259
2021 FS	CLE	MLB	30	2	2	5	57	0	50	44	8	2.7	9.7	53	37.5%	.285
2021 DC	CLE	MLB	30	2	2	5	53	0	57	51	9	2.7	9.7	61	37.5%	.285

Comparables: Shawn Armstrong, Addison Reed, Emilio Pagán

There was a nasty surprise lurking beneath the shiny surface of Wittgren's ERA in his first season in Cleveland: he allowed the highest average exit velocity of any pitcher with at least 100 batted balls. That might have been the impetus behind a curious tweak to his pitch mix, one that saw him torn more to the pitch that allowed the hardest contact, his changeup. He didn't misread the printout; what he did was he found a little extra movement on the offering and generated a career-high whiff rate. Alas, that didn't cure Wittgren's problem with quality contact so much as it moved it to a different pitch: hitters teed off on the curve instead, albeit without it harming his ERA. Without more explosive stuff, he may always be a pitcher who gives up loud contact; of course, it may not matter if he can continue to evolve and continue to keep runs off the board.

YEAR	TEAM	LVL	AGE	WHIP	ERA	DRA-	WARP	MPH	FB%	WHF	CSP
2018	NO	AAA	27	1.43	5.22	61	0.8				
2018	MIA	MLB	27	1.31	2.94	85	0.4	93.9	70.1%	22.5%	
2019	CLE	MLB	28	1.08	2.81	100	0.3	93.9	66.4%	23.2%	
2020	CLE	MLB	29	1.01	3.42	101	0.2	94.5	60.7%	29.0%	
2021 FS	CLE	MLB	30	1.19	3.56	88	0.6	94.1	65.3%	24.9%	48.4%
2021 DC	CLE	MLB	30	1.19	3.56	88	0.7	94.1	65.3%	24.9%	48.4%

Nick Wittgren, continued

Pitch Shape vs LHH

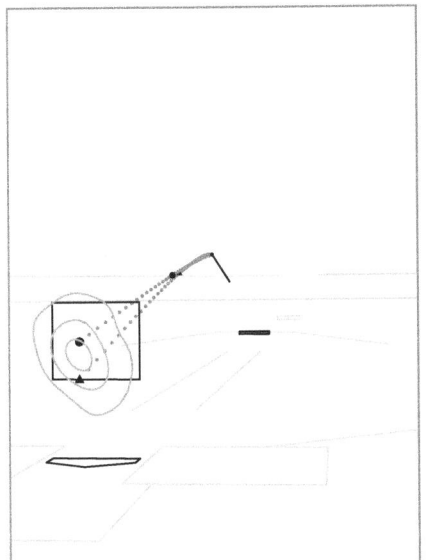

Pitch Shape vs RHH

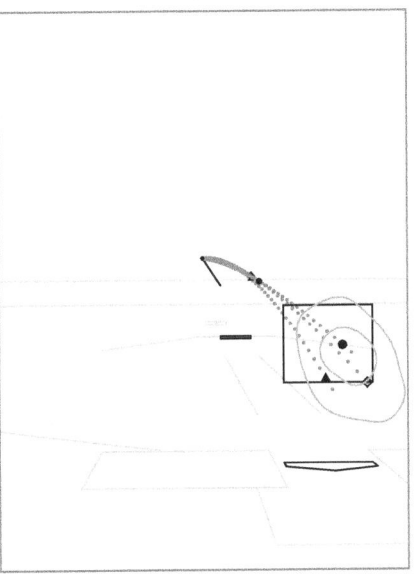

Type	Frequency	Velocity	H Movement	V Movement
● Fastball	59.5%	93.1 [101]	-8.8 [90]	-13.7 [104]
▲ Changeup	23.6%	86.3 [104]	-13.1 [92]	-30.6 [91]
◇ Curveball	14.8%	85.4 [127]	4.1 [86]	-33.5 [133]

PLAYER COMMENTS WITHOUT GRAPHS

Gabriel Arias SS
Born: 02/27/00   Age: 21   Bats: R   Throws: R
Height: 6'1"   Weight: 201   Origin: International Free Agent, 2016

YEAR	TEAM	LVL	AGE	PA	R	2B	3B	HR	RBI	BB	K	SB	CS	AVG/OBP/SLG
2018	FW	LO-A	18	504	54	27	3	6	55	41	149	3	3	.240/.302/.352
2019	LE	HI-A	19	506	62	21	4	17	75	24	126	8	4	.304/.341/.474
2021 FS	CLE	MLB	21	600	49	22	2	12	56	29	220	0	1	.207/.250/.325

Comparables: Franklin Barreto, Gleyber Torres, Xander Bogaerts

Arias is so tooled-up he could co-host with Tim Taylor. Someone shouted "MORE POWER!" on the set before the 2019 season, and he obliged by hitting 17 of his 23 career home runs. In true "Tool Time" fashion, there's no guarantee that the rest of Arias' tools—specifically his hit—will be used correctly, but he has a chance for four average or better offerings when all is said and done. Perhaps that's why the Padres felt comfortable shipping him off as part of the Mike Clevinger payout. Oh well. Arias can take solace in knowing he no longer has to sculpt ice using a chainsaw to garner attention, the way he did in San Diego's loaded system.

YEAR	TEAM	LVL	AGE	PA	DRC+	BABIP	BRR	FRAA	WARP
2018	FW	LO-A	18	504	84	.340	-0.5	SS(111): 6.2, 3B(6): 0.2	1.2
2019	LE	HI-A	19	506	121	.380	1.5	SS(104): -11.4, 3B(10): 1.4, 2B(2): -0.4	2.1
2021 FS	CLE	MLB	21	600	54	.313	-0.5	SS -1, 3B 0	-1.9

Jake Bauers LF

Born: 10/06/95 Age: 25 Bats: L Throws: L
Height: 6'1" Weight: 195 Origin: Round 7, 2013 Draft (#208 overall)

YEAR	TEAM	LVL	AGE	PA	R	2B	3B	HR	RBI	BB	K	SB	CS	AVG/OBP/SLG
2018	DUR	AAA	22	222	31	14	0	5	24	23	47	10	6	.279/.357/.426
2018	TB	MLB	22	388	48	22	2	11	48	54	104	6	6	.201/.316/.384
2019	COL	AAA	23	103	13	7	0	3	15	14	26	8	2	.247/.350/.427
2019	CLE	MLB	23	423	46	16	1	12	43	45	115	3	3	.226/.312/.371
2021 FS	CLE	MLB	25	600	70	25	1	19	66	71	154	5	3	.226/.325/.389
2021 DC	CLE	MLB	25	263	30	11	0	8	29	31	67	2	1	.226/.325/.389

Comparables: Mike Carp, Carlos Delgado, Derrek Lee

We apologize for going back to the well with the Jack Bauer references, but it's apparent that Bauers is...well, the anti-Bauer. Whereas Bauer gets the call in the most desperate of situations—assassination attempts, nuclear threats and poor primetime ad rates—Bauers went unsummoned despite Cleveland's outfield emergency. They employed 11 players as starting outfielders in 2020, yet he remained stored away at the Alternate Site like an unneeded bit character. Bauers *is* entering his age-24 season—ahem—so maybe there's some reason to hope that he can avert disaster. If he fails to make good on it, that ticking clock you'll hear will be counting down the hours until he's designated for assignment.

YEAR	TEAM	LVL	AGE	PA	DRC+	BABIP	BRR	FRAA	WARP
2018	DUR	AAA	22	222	124	.345	0.9	1B(46): -0.4, LF(4): 0.3, RF(2): -0.2	0.6
2018	TB	MLB	22	388	86	.252	2.5	1B(76): -2.4, LF(16): 0.5, RF(4): 0.0	0.0
2019	COL	AAA	23	103	95	.317	0.1	LF(15): 2.1, 1B(6): 0.1, CF(1): 0.0	0.3
2019	CLE	MLB	23	423	85	.290	0.7	LF(53): 0.1, 1B(31): -2.2	-0.1
2021 FS	CLE	MLB	25	600	95	.285	-0.4	1B -1, LF 0	0.6
2021 DC	CLE	MLB	25	263	95	.285	-0.2	1B 0	0.2

Bobby Bradley 1B

Born: 05/29/96 Age: 25 Bats: L Throws: R
Height: 6'1" Weight: 225 Origin: Round 3, 2014 Draft (#97 overall)

YEAR	TEAM	LVL	AGE	PA	R	2B	3B	HR	RBI	BB	K	SB	CS	AVG/OBP/SLG
2018	AKR	AA	22	421	49	19	3	24	64	45	105	1	0	.214/.304/.477
2018	COL	AAA	22	128	11	7	2	3	19	11	43	0	0	.254/.323/.430
2019	COL	AAA	23	453	65	23	0	33	74	46	153	0	0	.264/.344/.567
2019	CLE	MLB	23	49	4	5	0	1	4	4	20	0	0	.178/.245/.356
2021 FS	CLE	MLB	25	600	66	25	1	23	68	53	222	0	0	.200/.279/.382
2021 DC	CLE	MLB	25	226	25	9	0	8	25	20	83	0	0	.200/.279/.382

Comparables: Pete Alonso, Ryan O'Hearn, Jerry Sands

If your only positions are first base and designated hitter, and the big club employs Carlos Santana and Franmil Reyes, opportunities are going to be few and far between. Bradley received zero during the shortened season, so we're no closer to knowing whether his power can offset his swing-and-miss issues. Or, viewed from another perspective, maybe we are—he's likelier to hit the waiver-wire by the time you read this than lock down a spot.

YEAR	TEAM	LVL	AGE	PA	DRC+	BABIP	BRR	FRAA	WARP
2018	AKR	AA	22	421	106	.226	-2.3	1B(97): 1.4	0.0
2018	COL	AAA	22	128	99	.377	0.3	1B(29): 1.5	0.2
2019	COL	AAA	23	453	124	.336	-2.5	1B(98): 1.9	1.7
2019	CLE	MLB	23	49	53	.292	-0.1	1B(5): -0.2	-0.2
2021 FS	CLE	MLB	25	600	77	.289	-0.9	1B 1	-1.0
2021 DC	CLE	MLB	25	226	77	.289	-0.3	1B 0	-0.4

Yu Chang SS

Born: 08/18/95 Age: 25 Bats: R Throws: R
Height: 6'1" Weight: 180 Origin: International Free Agent, 2013

YEAR	TEAM	LVL	AGE	PA	R	2B	3B	HR	RBI	BB	K	SB	CS	AVG/OBP/SLG
2018	COL	AAA	22	518	56	28	2	13	62	44	144	4	3	.256/.330/.411
2019	COL	AAA	23	283	45	15	1	9	39	26	67	4	1	.253/.322/.427
2019	CLE	MLB	23	84	8	2	1	1	6	11	22	0	0	.178/.286/.274
2020	CLE	MLB	24	13	1	0	0	0	1	2	4	0	0	.182/.308/.182
2021 FS	CLE	MLB	25	600	66	21	3	19	64	52	190	2	1	.203/.284/.365
2021 DC	CLE	MLB	25	62	6	2	0	2	6	5	19	0	0	.203/.284/.365

Comparables: Brandon Wood, Edmundo Sosa, Matt Reynolds

Chang is caught in an awkward position. He's old enough to hold down a big-league roster spot on a permanent basis, but he can't seem to break through. Of the 240 available starts on Cleveland's dirt in 2020, 232 went to the same quartet that started on Opening Day. Just three of those starts found their way to Chang, who hasn't done much in his various cameos to warrant more. The problem with being old enough but seemingly not good enough for a major-league role is that, before long, you find yourself too old to be considered a prospect, then you find yourself out of chances. Calendar page by calendar page, Chang is inching closer to that fate.

YEAR	TEAM	LVL	AGE	PA	DRC+	BABIP	BRR	FRAA	WARP
2018	COL	AAA	22	518	102	.341	-3.3	SS(94): -7.3, 3B(23): -0.7, 2B(9): -0.9	0.3
2019	COL	AAA	23	283	92	.306	0.9	2B(23): 0.4, SS(22): 0.2, 3B(17): -0.7	0.8
2019	CLE	MLB	23	84	76	.240	-0.9	3B(25): -0.3, SS(8): -0.1	-0.1
2020	CLE	MLB	24	13	85	.286	-0.2	SS(4): 0.2, 3B(3): -0.1, 2B(2): 0.3	0.1
2021 FS	CLE	MLB	25	600	77	.274	-0.3	2B -1, 3B -1	-0.4
2021 DC	CLE	MLB	25	62	77	.274	0.0	2B 0, 3B 0	-0.1

Cleveland 2021

Mike Freeman 2B
Born: 08/04/87 Age: 33 Bats: L Throws: R
Height: 6'0" Weight: 195 Origin: Round 11, 2010 Draft (#331 overall)

YEAR	TEAM	LVL	AGE	PA	R	2B	3B	HR	RBI	BB	K	SB	CS	AVG/OBP/SLG
2018	IOW	AAA	30	330	51	15	2	6	38	25	66	6	6	.272/.328/.394
2018	CHC	MLB	30	1	0	0	0	0	0	0	0	0	0	None/None/None
2019	COL	AAA	31	33	6	0	0	3	3	9	7	1	0	.208/.424/.583
2019	CLE	MLB	31	213	27	8	0	4	24	22	61	1	2	.277/.362/.390
2020	CLE	MLB	32	43	5	3	0	0	3	3	11	0	0	.237/.302/.316
2021 FS	*CLE*	*MLB*	*33*	*600*	*56*	*17*	*1*	*12*	*56*	*52*	*168*	*1*	*1*	*.221/.296/.329*

Comparables: Mark Bellhorn, Mike Fontenot, Michael Martinez

The highlight of Freeman's 2020 was a tweet. You know the one, where he suggested that José Ramírez should have a higher WAR, an assessment he was uniquely qualified to make as the replacement in question. Give Freeman this much: he's self-aware. Give him this, too: he has outstanding taste in walk-up music, as his every plate appearance summons some premium Chris Stapleton. You know the one: *Say the word and he'll be there for you/J-Ram, Freeman will be your WAR's parachute.*

YEAR	TEAM	LVL	AGE	PA	DRC+	BABIP	BRR	FRAA	WARP
2018	IOW	AAA	30	330	100	.329	1.8	SS(55): 2.7, 2B(16): -0.1, CF(4): -0.4	1.4
2018	CHC	MLB	30	1	91			2B(1): -0.0	0.0
2019	COL	AAA	31	33	146	.143	0.0	SS(4): 0.2, 2B(2): 0.1, 3B(2): 0.2	0.3
2019	CLE	MLB	31	213	78	.388	1.3	2B(33): 2.1, 3B(18): -0.1, SS(9): -0.4	0.4
2020	CLE	MLB	32	43	89	.321	-0.1	3B(6): -0.2, 2B(4): -0.2, LF(4): 0.4	0.0
2021 FS	*CLE*	*MLB*	*33*	*600*	*73*	*.297*	*-0.6*	*SS 0, 2B 1*	*-0.2*

Tyler Freeman SS

Born: 05/21/99   Age: 22   Bats: R   Throws: R
Height: 6'0"   Weight: 170   Origin: Round 2, 2017 Draft (#71 overall)

YEAR	TEAM	LVL	AGE	PA	R	2B	3B	HR	RBI	BB	K	SB	CS	AVG/OBP/SLG
2018	MV	SS	19	301	49	29	4	2	38	8	22	14	3	.352/.405/.511
2019	LC	LO-A	20	272	51	16	3	3	24	18	28	11	4	.292/.382/.424
2019	LYN	HI-A	20	275	38	16	2	0	20	8	25	8	1	.319/.354/.397
2021 FS	CLE	MLB	22	600	67	28	2	7	56	30	97	9	4	.255/.315/.359
2021 DC	CLE	MLB	22	34	3	1	0	0	3	1	5	0	0	.255/.315/.359

Comparables: José Rondón, Wilmer Flores, Luis Sardiñas

For most prospects, the loss of the 2020 season meant an almost total absence of information. It only grew the legend of Freeman, who seemed to generate more buzz from the alternate site than anyone else. Sporadic Twitter reports—including from a family member—indicated that he was hitting for more power, producing at least eight home runs in game action. What any of that means when we don't know any of the other context, from number of plate appearances to most of the opposing pitchers, is much harder to say. What we *can* say—with confidence—is a vacancy will be opening up in Cleveland's infield soon, probably by the time you read this. Freeman is a prime candidate to claim it as his own before long.

YEAR	TEAM	LVL	AGE	PA	DRC+	BABIP	BRR	FRAA	WARP
2018	MV	SS	19	301	180	.372	3.5	SS(52): -0.1, 2B(10): -0.2	2.7
2019	LC	LO-A	20	272	141	.320	2.6	SS(57): 0.5, 2B(3): -0.2	2.6
2019	LYN	HI-A	20	275	129	.350	1.2	SS(57): -1.0, 2B(3): 0.1	1.9
2021 FS	CLE	MLB	22	600	87	.299	0.3	SS 2, 2B 0	1.0
2021 DC	CLE	MLB	22	34	87	.299	0.0	SS 0	0.1

Cleveland 2021

Billy Hamilton CF
Born: 09/09/90 Age: 30 Bats: S Throws: R
Height: 6'0" Weight: 155 Origin: Round 2, 2009 Draft (#57 overall)

YEAR	TEAM	LVL	AGE	PA	R	2B	3B	HR	RBI	BB	K	SB	CS	AVG/OBP/SLG
2018	CIN	MLB	27	556	74	16	9	4	29	46	132	34	10	.236/.299/.327
2019	KC	MLB	28	305	32	12	2	0	12	25	74	18	5	.211/.275/.269
2019	ATL	MLB	28	48	9	2	0	0	3	7	13	4	1	.268/.375/.317
2020	CHC	MLB	29	11	6	0	0	1	1	1	4	3	1	.300/.364/.600
2020	NYM	MLB	29	25	4	0	0	0	1	1	3	3	1	.045/.083/.045
2021 FS	CLE	MLB	30	600	50	17	3	8	51	49	141	45	12	.220/.287/.312

Comparables: Cecil Espy, Herm Winningham, Chris Duffy

Since being selected off waivers by Atlanta from Kansas City in August 2019, Hamilton has been employed by four different franchises and has accumulated 120 plate appearances and 16 stolen bases. He sure can fly...and he'll have to continue doing so at his usual rate to avoid changing teams.

YEAR	TEAM	LVL	AGE	PA	DRC+	BABIP	BRR	FRAA	WARP
2018	CIN	MLB	27	556	70	.309	8.3	CF(150): 4.2	1.2
2019	KC	MLB	28	305	55	.286	4.0	CF(90): -2.9	-0.5
2019	ATL	MLB	28	48	82	.393	0.5	CF(24): -2.7	-0.2
2020	CHC	MLB	29	11	80	.400	0.7	CF(12): -0.2	0.0
2020	NYM	MLB	29	25	87	.050	0.1	CF(13): -1.0	0.0
2021 FS	CLE	MLB	30	600	64	.282	4.4	CF 4	0.0

Daniel Johnson RF
Born: 07/11/95 Age: 25 Bats: L Throws: L
Height: 5'10" Weight: 200 Origin: Round 5, 2016 Draft (#154 overall)

YEAR	TEAM	LVL	AGE	PA	R	2B	3B	HR	RBI	BB	K	SB	CS	AVG/OBP/SLG
2018	HBG	AA	22	391	48	19	7	6	31	23	90	21	4	.267/.321/.410
2019	AKR	AA	23	167	25	7	2	10	33	16	39	6	3	.253/.337/.534
2019	COL	AAA	23	380	51	27	5	9	44	34	79	6	7	.306/.371/.496
2020	CLE	MLB	24	13	0	0	0	0	0	1	5	0	0	.083/.154/.083
2021 FS	CLE	MLB	25	600	67	25	3	18	72	39	168	10	5	.232/.296/.395
2021 DC	CLE	MLB	25	196	22	8	1	6	23	12	54	3	2	.232/.296/.395

Comparables: Wladimir Balentien, Ben Francisco, Corey Hart

For as bad as Cleveland's outfield was, it's disappointing that the toolsy, oft-injured Johnson was provided only 13 plate appearances to provide a jolt. Considering the brevity of the sample, we'll err on the optimistic side and say Cleveland just wanted to get a look at their older options rather than it being an indictment on Johnson and his long-term prospects.

YEAR	TEAM	LVL	AGE	PA	DRC+	BABIP	BRR	FRAA	WARP
2018	HBG	AA	22	391	95	.338	-2.3	RF(54): 6.3, CF(33): -2.9, LF(4): -0.7	0.2
2019	AKR	AA	23	167	121	.276	-2.3	CF(24): -2.3, RF(10): -0.3, LF(4): -0.6	0.2
2019	COL	AAA	23	380	122	.370	-1.5	RF(48): 6.4, CF(21): 1.2, LF(9): 0.0	2.4
2020	CLE	MLB	24	13	77	.143		RF(4): -0.6, LF(1): -0.1	-0.1
2021 FS	CLE	MLB	25	600	86	.301	0.8	RF 10, LF 0	1.6
2021 DC	CLE	MLB	25	196	86	.301	0.3	RF 3	0.4

Nolan Jones 3B

Born: 05/07/98 Age: 23 Bats: L Throws: R
Height: 6'2" Weight: 185 Origin: Round 2, 2016 Draft (#55 overall)

YEAR	TEAM	LVL	AGE	PA	R	2B	3B	HR	RBI	BB	K	SB	CS	AVG/OBP/SLG
2018	LC	LO-A	20	389	46	12	0	16	49	63	97	2	1	.279/.393/.464
2018	LYN	HI-A	20	130	23	9	0	3	17	26	34	0	0	.298/.438/.471
2019	LYN	HI-A	21	324	48	12	1	7	41	65	84	5	3	.286/.435/.425
2019	AKR	AA	21	211	33	10	2	8	22	31	63	2	0	.253/.370/.466
2021 FS	CLE	MLB	23	600	74	22	2	16	60	68	217	0	1	.217/.310/.364
2021 DC	CLE	MLB	23	136	16	5	0	3	13	15	49	0	0	.217/.310/.364

Comparables: Austin Riley, Matt Davidson, Tyler O'Neill

Jones' defense at third base is not why the team is excited about adding him to the lineup. Rather, he's been projected to slide away from the hot corner for most of his pro career. That might happen before he takes a grounder in the big leagues, with Cleveland giving him some reps in the outfield at fall instructs. Lord knows they could use Jones' bat in the lineup as soon as possible.

YEAR	TEAM	LVL	AGE	PA	DRC+	BABIP	BRR	FRAA	WARP
2018	LC	LO-A	20	389	150	.347	-0.9	3B(76): -4.1	2.3
2018	LYN	HI-A	20	130	154	.418	0.1	3B(28): -0.3	0.9
2019	LYN	HI-A	21	324	172	.396	-1.4	3B(72): -3.4	2.8
2019	AKR	AA	21	211	149	.346	0.8	3B(44): 0.0	1.8
2021 FS	CLE	MLB	23	600	85	.333	-0.7	3B 0	-0.1
2021 DC	CLE	MLB	23	136	85	.333	-0.2	3B 0, RF 0	0.0

Cleveland 2021

Leonys Martin CF
Born: 03/06/88   Age: 33   Bats: L   Throws: R
Height: 6'2"   Weight: 200   Origin: International Free Agent, 2011

YEAR	TEAM	LVL	AGE	PA	R	2B	3B	HR	RBI	BB	K	SB	CS	AVG/OBP/SLG
2018	DET	MLB	30	336	45	15	3	9	29	29	75	7	3	.251/.321/.409
2018	CLE	MLB	30	17	3	0	0	2	4	1	2	0	1	.333/.353/.733
2019	CHB	NPB	31	228	32	9	0	14	39	26	57	3	3	.232/.342/.495
2019	CLE	MLB	31	264	32	7	0	9	19	21	78	4	5	.199/.276/.343
2020	CHB	NPB	32	448	72	15	0	25	65	70	100	7	2	.234/.382/.485
2021 FS	CLE	MLB	33	600	60	23	2	17	66	44	169	19	7	.224/.290/.373

Comparables: Pete Whisenant, Cameron Maybin, Devon White

In his first full season with Lotte, the cannon-armed Cuban led the team in home runs, runs scored, and ISO. Martín's 25 long balls marked the second-highest total by a Marine in the last 15 years, trailing only Brandon Laird in 2019, and the most by a left-handed Lotte hitter since Seung-Yuop Lee, who hit 30 taters all the way back in 2005. That story tells you two things; a) the Marines have traditionally been power-deprived since they moved across the Tokyo Bay, from Kawasaki to Makuhari, in 1992; and b) Martín has enjoyed a power surge in his 1.5 years in Japan. In fact, Martín ranked fifth on the team in homers in 2019 despite playing his first game with them in late July. He has now walloped two-thirds of his MLB career home run total, and in under a quarter of the plate appearances. It puts him on track to hit the other third by the end of August 2021, having inked an extension that will keep him in Chiba for two more years.

YEAR	TEAM	LVL	AGE	PA	DRC+	BABIP	BRR	FRAA	WARP
2018	DET	MLB	30	336	100	.305	0.7	CF(74): 18.5	3.2
2018	CLE	MLB	30	17	98	.250	0.4	CF(5): 0.1, RF(1): -0.0	0.1
2019	CHB	NPB	31	228					
2019	CLE	MLB	31	264	70	.255	0.7	CF(65): 2.7	0.3
2020	CHB	NPB	32	448					
2021 FS	CLE	MLB	33	600	80	.291	1.6	CF 14, RF 0	1.9

Oscar Mercado RF

Born: 12/16/94   Age: 26   Bats: R   Throws: R
Height: 6'2"   Weight: 197   Origin: Round 2, 2013 Draft (#57 overall)

YEAR	TEAM	LVL	AGE	PA	R	2B	3B	HR	RBI	BB	K	SB	CS	AVG/OBP/SLG
2018	COL	AAA	23	119	12	5	1	0	5	13	23	6	4	.252/.342/.320
2018	MEM	AAA	23	427	73	21	1	8	42	36	64	31	8	.285/.351/.408
2019	COL	AAA	24	140	24	10	1	4	15	16	32	14	3	.294/.396/.496
2019	CLE	MLB	24	482	70	25	3	15	54	28	84	15	4	.269/.318/.443
2020	CLE	MLB	25	93	6	1	0	1	6	5	27	3	0	.128/.174/.174
2021 FS	CLE	MLB	26	600	69	26	2	15	63	41	142	21	9	.235/.298/.378
2021 DC	CLE	MLB	26	325	37	14	1	8	34	22	76	11	5	.235/.298/.378

Comparables: Devon White, Billy Conigliaro, Luis Matos

As sequels go, Mercado's sophomore effort was the worst since *Speed 2: Cruise Control*. It made about an equal amount of sense. Mercado's performance was so lifeless that even Jason Patric could emulate it. The action sequences he orchestrated on the basepaths and in the field that made him a hit in the first place were still present, but they were fewer in number and harder to get amped up about with the sheer dross he offered at the plate. Cleveland banished him from the limelight by mid-August, yet he seemed no better when he returned for September. There's enough here to greenlight a third installment. After that, we'll see.

YEAR	TEAM	LVL	AGE	PA	DRC+	BABIP	BRR	FRAA	WARP
2018	COL	AAA	23	119	94	.325	-2.2	CF(24): -0.8, RF(7): 0.3, LF(1): 0.1	-0.1
2018	MEM	AAA	23	427	108	.323	8.1	CF(89): -2.6, LF(7): -0.5, RF(2): -0.1	1.8
2019	COL	AAA	24	140	129	.373	1.1	CF(19): 5.4, LF(5): 1.1, RF(4): 0.2	1.5
2019	CLE	MLB	24	482	97	.300	2.3	CF(82): 8.3, LF(24): -1.6, RF(9): -1.1	2.2
2020	CLE	MLB	25	93	61	.169	0.9	CF(21): 3.8, LF(12): 0.3	0.2
2021 FS	CLE	MLB	26	600	83	.291	1.7	CF 8, LF 0	1.5
2021 DC	CLE	MLB	26	325	83	.291	0.9	CF 4	0.9

Owen Miller SS

Born: 11/15/96 Age: 24 Bats: R Throws: R
Height: 5'11" Weight: 197 Origin: Round 3, 2018 Draft (#84 overall)

YEAR	TEAM	LVL	AGE	PA	R	2B	3B	HR	RBI	BB	K	SB	CS	AVG/OBP/SLG
2018	TRI	SS	21	216	22	8	3	2	20	15	24	4	4	.335/.395/.440
2018	FW	LO-A	21	114	18	11	0	2	13	4	17	0	0	.336/.368/.495
2019	AMA	AA	22	560	76	28	2	13	68	46	86	5	5	.290/.355/.430
2021 FS	CLE	MLB	24	600	57	26	2	12	61	37	130	1	1	.249/.305/.375

Comparables: Gregorio Petit, Chris Valaika, Eugenio Suárez

Both Cleveland shortstop prospect archetypes came over in the Clevinger deal. Along with a raw, projectable high-ceiling type in Arias, they received Miller, a polished hitter with advanced bat-to-ball skills who's likely to be contributing in the majors sometime in 2021.

YEAR	TEAM	LVL	AGE	PA	DRC+	BABIP	BRR	FRAA	WARP
2018	TRI	SS	21	216	158	.369	-2.5	SS(43): 3.3	1.4
2018	FW	LO-A	21	114	134	.382	0.9	3B(13): -2.8, SS(7): -0.4	0.4
2019	AMA	AA	22	560	112	.328	1.3	SS(71): 5.1, 2B(48): 0.5, 3B(6): -0.3	3.4
2021 FS	CLE	MLB	24	600	86	.305	-0.7	SS 1, 2B 1	0.7

Tyler Naquin RF

Born: 04/24/91 Age: 30 Bats: L Throws: R
Height: 6'2" Weight: 195 Origin: Round 1, 2012 Draft (#15 overall)

YEAR	TEAM	LVL	AGE	PA	R	2B	3B	HR	RBI	BB	K	SB	CS	AVG/OBP/SLG
2018	CLE	MLB	27	183	22	7	0	3	23	6	42	1	1	.264/.295/.356
2019	CLE	MLB	28	294	34	19	0	10	34	14	66	4	2	.288/.325/.467
2020	CLE	MLB	29	141	15	8	1	4	20	5	40	0	1	.218/.248/.383
2021 FS	CLE	MLB	30	600	63	28	2	19	71	44	170	5	3	.243/.306/.410

Comparables: Cory Snyder, Jay Bruce, Clete Thomas

The 60-game season left us onlookers more desperate than usual for indicators of surprise breakouts. A combination of small-sample theater and the dire state of the Cleveland offense conspired to cast Naquin in the shockingly premature role of offensive savior. He recovered from a toe fracture to quickly become an everyday player by producing the second-best OPS in a lineup that could hardly be bothered to field more than a few capable sticks at a time. That was 20 games in; by the time that sample doubled, it was obvious that he was not an emerging offensive juggernaut, or even a reliable above-average bat. He was simply the same Tyler Naquin who seems incapable of producing at a tolerable level for long.

YEAR	TEAM	LVL	AGE	PA	DRC+	BABIP	BRR	FRAA	WARP
2018	CLE	MLB	27	183	78	.331	1.0	RF(39): 5.2, CF(19): 0.2, LF(5): -0.4	0.6
2019	CLE	MLB	28	294	93	.345	-0.3	RF(68): 12.2, LF(15): 4.1	2.0
2020	CLE	MLB	29	141	75	.275	-0.3	RF(39): 1.9	0.2
2021 FS	CLE	MLB	30	600	92	.318	-0.1	RF 10, CF 2	2.2

Bo Naylor C

Born: 02/21/00 Age: 21 Bats: L Throws: R
Height: 6'0" Weight: 195 Origin: Round 1, 2018 Draft (#29 overall)

YEAR	TEAM	LVL	AGE	PA	R	2B	3B	HR	RBI	BB	K	SB	CS	AVG/OBP/SLG
2018	INDB	ROK	18	139	17	3	3	2	17	21	28	5	1	.274/.381/.402
2019	LC	LO-A	19	453	60	18	10	11	65	43	104	7	5	.243/.313/.421
2021 FS	CLE	MLB	21	600	49	21	5	11	54	41	191	4	3	.204/.262/.324

Comparables: Jorge Alfaro, Joe Benson, Greg Golson

The unconventional season might have accelerated Naylor's development in at least one regard: it afforded him the opportunity to work with more advanced pitchers than he'd have encountered in A-ball. He doesn't need to rush to ensure a family reunion, either, as recently-acquired brother Josh is set to be in the organization for the next half-decade.

YEAR	TEAM	LVL	AGE	PA	DRC+	BABIP	BRR	FRAA	WARP
2018	INDB	ROK	18	139		.341			
2019	LC	LO-A	19	453	97	.296	0.9	C(85): 3.4	2.2
2021 FS	CLE	MLB	21	600	61	.290	0.5	C 1, 3B 0	-0.5

Josh Naylor RF

Born: 06/22/97 Age: 24 Bats: L Throws: L
Height: 5'11" Weight: 250 Origin: Round 1, 2015 Draft (#12 overall)

YEAR	TEAM	LVL	AGE	PA	R	2B	3B	HR	RBI	BB	K	SB	CS	AVG/OBP/SLG
2018	SA	AA	21	574	72	22	1	17	74	64	69	5	5	.297/.383/.447
2019	ELP	AAA	22	252	51	20	1	10	42	28	30	1	0	.314/.389/.547
2019	SD	MLB	22	279	29	15	0	8	32	25	64	1	1	.249/.315/.403
2020	SD	MLB	23	38	4	0	1	1	4	1	4	1	0	.278/.316/.417
2020	CLE	MLB	23	66	9	3	0	0	2	4	8	0	0	.230/.277/.279
2021 FS	*CLE*	*MLB*	*24*	*600*	*69*	*29*	*1*	*18*	*68*	*48*	*114*	*2*	*2*	*.256/.321/.417*
2021 DC	*CLE*	*MLB*	*24*	*366*	*42*	*17*	*1*	*11*	*41*	*29*	*69*	*1*	*1*	*.256/.321/.417*

Comparables: Domonic Brown, Geoff Jenkins, Alex Gordon

If Tyler Naquin's rise and fall was exaggerated because of the 60-game campaign, Naylor took the effect to another level by erasing a season of poor production with a single game. He did nothing to spark life into the moribund Cleveland outfield upon arriving from San Diego, failing to hit a homer in a Cleveland uniform—until the playoffs, that is. Naylor marked his postseason debut with four hits in Game 1 of the American League Wild Card Series, with three of those coming against Gerrit Cole. He later became the first player in history to record a hit in his first five postseason plate appearances when he doubled in Game 2. The decision to pinch-hit for him during the final frames of that contest sparked so much ire that one might have thought his season-long line resembled that of Ted Williams and not...well, himself. To be clear, Naylor is young and talented enough for this to represent a turning point. The challenge for him is to have his monster raw power and his impressive contact skills align more frequently. He should get the chance as Cleveland's regular first baseman.

YEAR	TEAM	LVL	AGE	PA	DRC+	BABIP	BRR	FRAA	WARP
2018	SA	AA	21	574	138	.317	-5.1	LF(89): -20.4, 1B(29): 0.6	-0.4
2019	ELP	AAA	22	252	117	.326	0.0	RF(29): -2.2, LF(22): 1.0	1.0
2019	SD	MLB	22	279	81	.302	-0.2	LF(33): 0.7, RF(31): -4.1	-0.3
2020	SD	MLB	23	38	84	.290	0.4	RF(4): -0.4, 1B(3): 0.2, LF(3): -0.0	0.0
2020	CLE	MLB	23	66	82	.264	1.6	LF(19): -0.6, 1B(2): -0.0	0.1
2021 FS	*CLE*	*MLB*	*24*	*600*	*100*	*.294*	*-0.7*	*1B 2, LF -1*	*1.4*
2021 DC	*CLE*	*MLB*	*24*	*366*	*100*	*.294*	*-0.4*	*1B 1, LF 0*	*0.6*

Yasiel Puig RF

Born: 12/07/90 Age: 30 Bats: R Throws: R
Height: 6'2" Weight: 240 Origin: International Free Agent, 2012

YEAR	TEAM	LVL	AGE	PA	R	2B	3B	HR	RBI	BB	K	SB	CS	AVG/OBP/SLG
2018	LAD	MLB	27	444	60	21	1	23	63	36	87	15	5	.267/.327/.494
2019	CLE	MLB	28	207	25	15	1	2	23	21	44	5	2	.297/.377/.423
2019	CIN	MLB	28	404	51	15	1	22	61	23	89	14	5	.252/.302/.475
2021 FS	CLE	MLB	30	600	69	25	1	21	75	54	135	14	7	.252/.325/.430
2021 DC	CLE	MLB	30	425	48	18	1	15	53	38	96	9	5	.252/.325/.430

Comparables: Larry Walker, Matt Joyce, Jason Lane

Since his debut with the Dodgers in 2013, Cuban émigré Puig has been one of the most polarizing players. His talent is undeniable—when healthy and on his game, he's one the few genuine five-tool players in the majors. Off the field, his eccentricities have rubbed some clubhouses, writers and fans the wrong way, though much of this opprobrium reads as thinly-veiled racism toward a player, and personality, that refuses to fall in line with the normative expectations of "traditional" (read: white) baseball culture. Unfortunately, there was no on-field Puig in 2020 to remind us of the good times, and Puig only made the news in more troubling ways. A COVID-19 infection nullified a contract agreement with Atlanta, and even more disturbing, in October Puig was sued by a woman claiming that the then-Dodger sexually assaulted her at a Lakers game in 2018. Puig's future has never been less certain, but the skills should be intact, presuming he can find a team willing to show them off to the best effect.

YEAR	TEAM	LVL	AGE	PA	DRC+	BABIP	BRR	FRAA	WARP
2018	LAD	MLB	27	444	120	.286	2.4	RF(118): -4.5	1.9
2019	CLE	MLB	28	207	101	.380	-1.5	RF(48): 2.7	0.6
2019	CIN	MLB	28	404	101	.272	-2.8	RF(98): 2.1	0.9
2021 FS	CLE	MLB	30	600	109	.296	0.7	RF 6	2.6
2021 DC	CLE	MLB	30	425	109	.296	0.5	RF 4	1.8

Cleveland 2021

Brayan Rocchio SS
Born: 01/13/01   Age: 20   Bats: S   Throws: R
Height: 5'10"   Weight: 150   Origin: International Free Agent, 2017

YEAR	TEAM	LVL	AGE	PA	R	2B	3B	HR	RBI	BB	K	SB	CS	AVG/OBP/SLG
2018	DSL IND1	ROK	17	111	19	2	3	1	12	5	14	8	5	.323/.391/.434
2018	INDB	ROK	17	158	21	10	1	1	17	10	17	14	8	.343/.389/.448
2019	MV	SS	18	295	33	12	3	5	27	20	40	14	8	.250/.310/.373
2021 FS	*CLE*	*MLB*	*20*	*600*	*49*	*23*	*3*	*9*	*53*	*27*	*139*	*21*	*12*	*.230/.272/.333*

Comparables: Sergio Alcántara, Willi Castro, Amed Rosario

If you were wondering where Cleveland's next compact, switch-hitting middle infielder with good contact skills was going to come from, Rocchio is a leading contender. He's not the *only* contender, but Cleveland is hardly likely to object if they end up with two in the lineup again.

YEAR	TEAM	LVL	AGE	PA	DRC+	BABIP	BRR	FRAA	WARP
2018	DSL IND1	ROK	17	111		.369			
2018	INDB	ROK	17	158		.378			
2019	MV	SS	18	295	106	.276	-1.8	SS(62): 5.5, 2B(7): 0.6	1.8
2021 FS	*CLE*	*MLB*	*20*	*600*	*64*	*.290*	*2.3*	*SS 4, 2B 0*	*-0.3*

Domingo Santana LF
Born: 08/05/92   Age: 28   Bats: R   Throws: R
Height: 6'5"   Weight: 232   Origin: International Free Agent, 2009

YEAR	TEAM	LVL	AGE	PA	R	2B	3B	HR	RBI	BB	K	SB	CS	AVG/OBP/SLG
2018	RMV	AAA	25	227	30	10	2	8	35	36	75	2	0	.283/.401/.487
2018	MIL	MLB	25	235	21	14	1	5	20	20	77	1	1	.265/.328/.412
2019	SEA	MLB	26	507	63	20	1	21	69	50	164	8	3	.253/.329/.441
2020	CLE	MLB	27	84	6	3	0	2	12	13	25	0	0	.157/.298/.286
2021 FS	*CLE*	*MLB*	*28*	*600*	*71*	*24*	*1*	*21*	*73*	*76*	*198*	*9*	*4*	*.231/.339/.410*

Comparables: Jay Buhner, Rob Deer, Jorge Soler

There's always something to cling on to with players like Santana, who need only a single moment to remind us what they're capable of doing. His time to shine came on August 8, when he obliterated a Steve Cishek sinker so thoroughly that it looked as though the ball might clear all of the seats in left-center. The problem with Santana is those awe-inspiring moments are happening less and less frequently. He slumped his way to an August DFA and will try to pick up the pieces with his fourth team in four years, this time the Yakult Swallows.

YEAR	TEAM	LVL	AGE	PA	DRC+	BABIP	BRR	FRAA	WARP
2018	RMV	AAA	25	227	123	.425	-2.6	RF(50): -10.4	-0.5
2018	MIL	MLB	25	235	82	.386	-0.2	RF(55): -2.0	-0.2
2019	SEA	MLB	26	507	101	.347	0.1	LF(59): -4.2, RF(42): -3.0	0.6
2020	CLE	MLB	27	84	80	.209	0.0	RF(16): 0.7, LF(9): 0.3	0.0
2021 FS	CLE	MLB	28	600	107	.331	0.0	RF -2, LF -1	1.6

Carson Tucker SS
Born: 01/24/02 Age: 19 Bats: R Throws: R
Height: 6'2" Weight: 180 Origin: Round 1, 2020 Draft (#23 overall)

As if graduating from high school during a pandemic wasn't stressful enough, Tucker has a whole lot else on his plate to manage. He was selected one pick earlier than his brother, Cole, but it's hard to brag about that sort of thing given that Cole is the one on a big-league roster. (Okay, so it's just the Pirates; still!) Tucker also has to hear about how he's the first shortstop Cleveland has taken in round one since 2011, when they snagged some youngster from Puerto Rico—Francisco something or another. Anyway, provided Tucker can block out all the noise around his selection, he should be able to develop into a well-rounded player who can win the sibling rivalry. As for topping the other guy? Well, there's no need to get greedy.

George Valera CF
Born: 11/13/00 Age: 20 Bats: L Throws: L
Height: 5'11" Weight: 185 Origin: International Free Agent, 2017

YEAR	TEAM	LVL	AGE	PA	R	2B	3B	HR	RBI	BB	K	SB	CS	AVG/OBP/SLG
2018	INDB	ROK	17	22	4	1	0	1	6	3	3	1	1	.333/.409/.556
2019	MV	SS	18	188	22	7	1	8	29	29	52	6	2	.236/.356/.446
2019	LC	LO-A	18	26	1	0	1	0	3	2	9	0	2	.087/.192/.174
2021 FS	CLE	MLB	20	600	48	21	2	12	54	40	217	9	8	.188/.248/.302

Comparables: Luis Alexander Basabe, Michael Saunders, Harold Ramirez

Valera may have signed in 2017, but he's been limited to fewer than 100 games played by injuries, careful management and now the pandemic. He has an All-Star ceiling and he just turned 20 in November, yet it's fair to wonder if all the starting and stopping will impact his long-term development.

YEAR	TEAM	LVL	AGE	PA	DRC+	BABIP	BRR	FRAA	WARP
2018	INDB	ROK	17	22		.333			
2019	MV	SS	18	188	132	.296	-0.3	CF(25): 0.7, RF(11): -3.5, LF(5): 4.4	1.1
2019	LC	LO-A	18	26	34	.143	-1.0	RF(3): 1.2, LF(2): 1.6	0.0
2021 FS	CLE	MLB	20	600	50	.283	1.0	CF 1, RF 0	-1.9

Bradley Zimmer CF

Born: 11/27/92 Age: 28 Bats: L Throws: R
Height: 6'5" Weight: 220 Origin: Round 1, 2014 Draft (#21 overall)

YEAR	TEAM	LVL	AGE	PA	R	2B	3B	HR	RBI	BB	K	SB	CS	AVG/OBP/SLG
2018	COL	AAA	25	28	1	0	0	1	1	1	11	1	0	.148/.179/.259
2018	CLE	MLB	25	114	14	5	0	2	9	7	44	4	1	.226/.281/.330
2019	COL	AAA	26	26	5	1	1	1	2	3	6	2	0	.364/.440/.636
2019	CLE	MLB	26	14	1	0	0	0	0	1	7	0	0	.000/.071/.000
2020	CLE	MLB	27	50	3	0	0	1	3	7	14	2	1	.162/.360/.243
2021 FS	CLE	MLB	28	600	70	17	2	17	58	60	206	23	6	.204/.305/.347
2021 DC	CLE	MLB	28	235	27	6	1	6	22	23	80	8	3	.204/.305/.347

Comparables: Chad Hermansen, Kirk Nieuwenhuis, Ryan Thompson

No one would tempt fate as to suggest Zimmer was in the best shape of his life when the 2020 season began. He was, however, in the kind of shape that allowed him to play baseball, which has seldom been the case for much of his recent career. Zimmer's body didn't betray him, either, even if the season did. As a player sorely in need of reps (he's taken fewer than 300 trips to the plate across the past three years), the cancellation of the minor-league season was a huge blow. He was, in turn, thrown back in at the big-league side of things in order to get his hacks—and yes, that's the operative word for what he did, as he recorded more strikeouts than hits-plus-walks. The most disappointing part of these seemingly interminable career interruptions might be that if Zimmer ever does put together another full season, it'll be without the full power of the physical gifts that used to tantalize us, evaluators and fans alike.

YEAR	TEAM	LVL	AGE	PA	DRC+	BABIP	BRR	FRAA	WARP
2018	COL	AAA	25	28	15	.200	0.1	CF(5): -0.2	-0.2
2018	CLE	MLB	25	114	48	.367	1.4	CF(34): 5.4	0.4
2019	COL	AAA	26	26	112	.467	0.6	CF(6): -0.1	0.2
2019	CLE	MLB	26	14	71	.000	0.3	RF(4): -0.4, CF(2): 0.2	0.0
2020	CLE	MLB	27	50	103	.217	-0.6	LF(8): -0.2, CF(7): -0.0, RF(7): -0.4	-0.1
2021 FS	CLE	MLB	28	600	81	.298	1.9	CF 3, RF -7	0.2
2021 DC	CLE	MLB	28	235	81	.298	0.7	CF 1, RF -3	0.0

Logan Allen LHP

Born: 05/23/97   Age: 24   Bats: R   Throws: L
Height: 6'3"   Weight: 220   Origin: Round 8, 2015 Draft (#231 overall)

YEAR	TEAM	LVL	AGE	W	L	SV	G	GS	IP	H	HR	BB/9	K/9	K	GB%	BABIP
2018	SA	AA	21	10	6	0	20	19	121	89	7	2.8	9.3	125	42.6%	.270
2018	ELP	AAA	21	4	0	0	5	5	27^2	21	4	4.2	8.5	26	36.8%	.236
2019	ELP	AAA	22	4	3	0	13	13	57^2	61	8	3.4	9.8	63	45.5%	.340
2019	COL	AAA	22	1	1	0	5	5	22^1	31	6	4.8	7.3	18	21.3%	.368
2019	SD	MLB	22	2	3	0	8	4	25^1	33	4	4.6	5.0	14	51.7%	.349
2019	CLE	MLB	22	0	0	0	1	0	2^1	3	0	0.0	11.6	3	16.7%	.500
2020	CLE	MLB	23	0	0	0	3	0	10^2	12	1	5.9	5.9	7	47.1%	.333
2021 FS	CLE	MLB	24	8	10	0	26	26	150	160	26	4.5	7.8	130	42.4%	.307
2021 DC	CLE	MLB	24	7	8	0	33	22	115.7	124	20	4.5	7.8	100	42.4%	.307

Comparables: Génesis Cabrera, JoJo Romero, Caleb Ferguson

Allen's time with Cleveland can be summed up in a word: anonymity. He wasn't the biggest name moved in the three-way trade that landed him with the Fightin' Franconas, nor has he been the most omnipresent in the year and a half since. His 2020 season comprised three low-leverage, mop-up relief appearances, making him four-for-four in that regard for his Cleveland career. To make matters worse, Cleveland used its second-round pick on a left-handed pitcher named...Logan Allen. Given the Younger Allen's polish, and the Older Allen's invisibility, it's possible he isn't even the best Logan Allen in the organization anymore.

YEAR	TEAM	LVL	AGE	WHIP	ERA	DRA-	WARP	MPH	FB%	WHF	CSP
2018	SA	AA	21	1.05	2.75	67	2.8				
2018	ELP	AAA	21	1.23	1.63	132	-0.2				
2019	ELP	AAA	22	1.44	5.15	78	1.6				
2019	COL	AAA	22	1.93	7.66	174	-0.4				
2019	SD	MLB	22	1.82	6.75	137	-0.3	95.1	48.7%	21.7%	
2019	CLE	MLB	22	1.29	0.00	168	-0.1	95.8	42.5%	21.7%	
2020	CLE	MLB	23	1.78	3.38	134	-0.1	95.4	45.7%	24.3%	
2021 FS	CLE	MLB	24	1.57	5.47	119	-0.2	95.3	47.2%	22.7%	47.3%
2021 DC	CLE	MLB	24	1.57	5.47	119	-0.4	95.3	47.2%	22.7%	47.3%

Cleveland 2021

Tanner Burns RHP
Born: 12/28/98   Age: 22   Bats: R   Throws: R
Height: 6'0"   Weight: 215   Origin: Round 1, 2020 Draft (#36 overall)

Burns is the kind of polished, low-frills pitcher Cleveland seems to extract more from than other organizations. He slid in the draft because of injury concerns, but if he can stay healthy then don't be surprised if he's quick to rise—and long to stay—in a big-league rotation.

Joey Cantillo LHP
Born: 12/18/99   Age: 21   Bats: L   Throws: L
Height: 6'4"   Weight: 220   Origin: Round 16, 2017 Draft (#468 overall)

YEAR	TEAM	LVL	AGE	W	L	SV	G	GS	IP	H	HR	BB/9	K/9	K	GB%	BABIP
2018	SD2	ROK	18	2	2	0	11	9	45^1	33	0	2.4	11.5	58	57.3%	.303
2018	FW	LO-A	18	0	1	0	1	1	3^2	4	0	7.4	12.3	5	70.0%	.400
2019	FW	LO-A	19	9	3	0	19	19	98	58	3	2.5	11.7	127	42.7%	.264
2019	LE	HI-A	19	1	1	0	3	3	13^2	12	2	4.6	10.5	16	38.5%	.270
2021 FS	CLE	MLB	21	2	2	0	57	0	50	43	7	4.6	9.8	54	42.8%	.283

Comparables: Tyler Danish, Miguel Castro, José Fernández

Underwhelming fastball? Check. Minimal prospect hype? Check? Gets by on deception and pitchability? Check. Cantillo's upside is probably back-end starter, but that tag comes with significant subtext now that he's relocated from San Diego to Cleveland.

YEAR	TEAM	LVL	AGE	WHIP	ERA	DRA-	WARP	MPH	FB%	WHF	CSP
2018	SD2	ROK	18	0.99	2.18						
2018	FW	LO-A	18	1.91	9.82	89	0.0				
2019	FW	LO-A	19	0.87	1.93	44	3.5				
2019	LE	HI-A	19	1.39	4.61	77	0.2				
2021 FS	CLE	MLB	21	1.38	4.06	100	0.2				

Emmanuel Clase RHP
Born: 03/18/98 Age: 23 Bats: R Throws: R
Height: 6'2" Weight: 206 Origin: International Free Agent, 2015

YEAR	TEAM	LVL	AGE	W	L	SV	G	GS	IP	H	HR	BB/9	K/9	K	GB%	BABIP
2018	SPO	SS	20	1	1	12	22	0	28[1]	16	0	1.9	8.6	27	61.1%	.225
2019	DE	HI-A	21	2	0	1	6	0	7	4	0	1.3	14.1	11	76.9%	.308
2019	FRI	AA	21	1	2	11	33	1	37[2]	34	1	1.9	9.3	39	61.3%	.317
2019	TEX	MLB	21	2	3	1	21	1	23[1]	20	2	2.3	8.1	21	59.1%	.281
2021 FS	CLE	MLB	23	2	2	3	57	0	50	47	6	4.0	8.7	48	52.9%	.298
2021 DC	CLE	MLB	23	2	2	3	53	0	57	54	6	4.0	8.7	55	52.9%	.298

Comparables: Yennsy Diaz, Carlos Sanabria, Germán Márquez

Whatever expectations were created by Clase headlining the Corey Kluber trade, it's safe to say that missing the entire season wasn't among them. The former Ranger looked to be among those who benefited from the late start to the schedule, giving him extra time to recover from the teres major strain that would have cost him a month or two of the season. His subsequent suspension for a positive boldenone test not only negated that advantage, but ultimately ensured he wouldn't make a big-league appearance in 2020. Cleveland will still have plenty of time to see if Clase and his triple-digit velocity and nasty cutter can make someone in the trade a winner.

YEAR	TEAM	LVL	AGE	WHIP	ERA	DRA-	WARP	MPH	FB%	WHF	CSP
2018	SPO	SS	20	0.78	0.64	241	-2.2				
2019	DE	HI-A	21	0.71	0.00	61	0.1				
2019	FRI	AA	21	1.12	3.35	76	0.4				
2019	TEX	MLB	21	1.11	2.31	80	0.4	101.0	78.8%	25.6%	
2021 FS	CLE	MLB	23	1.39	4.06	96	0.4	101.0	78.8%	25.6%	49.4%
2021 DC	CLE	MLB	23	1.39	4.06	96	0.4	101.0	78.8%	25.6%	49.4%

Daniel Espino RHP
Born: 01/05/01 Age: 20 Bats: R Throws: R
Height: 6'2" Weight: 205 Origin: Round 1, 2019 Draft (#24 overall)

YEAR	TEAM	LVL	AGE	W	L	SV	G	GS	IP	H	HR	BB/9	K/9	K	GB%	BABIP
2019	INDR	ROK	18	0	1	0	6	6	13[2]	7	1	3.3	10.5	16	48.4%	.207
2019	MV	SS	18	0	2	0	3	3	10	9	1	4.5	16.2	18	31.8%	.381
2021 FS	CLE	MLB	20	2	3	0	57	0	50	45	8	6.3	9.7	54	37.3%	.289

Espino was brought along slowly after being drafted and 2020, unsurprisingly, did little to change that. The 20-year-old flamethrower will have less than 25 pro innings to his name at the time of publication, so this is a key year for determining whether he can translate his exciting arsenal into at least a mid-rotation ceiling.

Cleveland 2021

YEAR	TEAM	LVL	AGE	WHIP	ERA	DRA-	WARP	MPH	FB%	WHF	CSP
2019	INDR	ROK	18	0.88	1.98						
2019	MV	SS	18	1.40	6.30	60	0.3				
2021 FS	CLE	MLB	20	1.62	5.36	122	-0.4				

Ethan Hankins   RHP
Born: 05/23/00   Age: 21   Bats: R   Throws: R
Height: 6'6"   Weight: 200   Origin: Round 1, 2018 Draft (#35 overall)

YEAR	TEAM	LVL	AGE	W	L	SV	G	GS	IP	H	HR	BB/9	K/9	K	GB%	BABIP
2018	INDB	ROK	18	0	0	0	2	2	3	4	0	0.0	18.0	6	28.6%	.571
2019	MV	SS	19	0	0	0	9	8	38^2	23	1	4.2	10.0	43	55.1%	.253
2019	LC	LO-A	19	0	3	0	5	5	21^1	20	3	5.1	11.8	28	47.2%	.340
2021 FS	CLE	MLB	21	2	3	0	57	0	50	46	8	6.0	8.9	49	46.0%	.282

Comparables: Joe Ross, Pedro Avila, Edgar Olmos

The past year gave very little indication of whether Hankins can harness his crossfire delivery sufficiently for a rotation spot. Instead, the lasting image of his year will be the disbelieving laugh he uttered after being taken deep by Reds first-round outfielder Austin Hendrick in instructs.

YEAR	TEAM	LVL	AGE	WHIP	ERA	DRA-	WARP	MPH	FB%	WHF	CSP
2018	INDB	ROK	18	1.33	6.00						
2019	MV	SS	19	1.06	1.40	68	0.8				
2019	LC	LO-A	19	1.50	4.64	113	-0.1				
2021 FS	CLE	MLB	21	1.59	5.26	120	-0.3				

Sam Hentges   LHP
Born: 07/18/96   Age: 24   Bats: L   Throws: L
Height: 6'6"   Weight: 245   Origin: Round 4, 2014 Draft (#128 overall)

YEAR	TEAM	LVL	AGE	W	L	SV	G	GS	IP	H	HR	BB/9	K/9	K	GB%	BABIP
2018	LYN	HI-A	21	6	6	0	23	23	118^1	114	4	4.0	9.3	122	37.8%	.348
2019	AKR	AA	22	2	13	0	26	26	128^2	148	11	4.5	8.7	125	34.0%	.358
2021 FS	CLE	MLB	24	2	3	0	57	0	50	48	8	5.5	8.4	46	35.1%	.288
2021 DC	CLE	MLB	24	3	3	0	26	4	43	41	7	5.5	8.4	40	35.1%	.288

Comparables: Chris Flexen, Pedro Avila, Michael Fulmer

Hentges consistently bumped the upper-90s during spring training, raising eyebrows about what he could do in a relief role. That feels like a lifetime ago, we know. In due time, Hentges' attempts at starting will probably feel the same way—especially if he keeps pumping that gas as a seventh-inning type.

YEAR	TEAM	LVL	AGE	WHIP	ERA	DRA-	WARP	MPH	FB%	WHF	CSP
2018	LYN	HI-A	21	1.41	3.27	84	1.9				
2019	AKR	AA	22	1.65	5.11	146	-3.4				
2021 FS	CLE	MLB	24	1.58	5.14	116	-0.2				
2021 DC	CLE	MLB	24	1.58	5.14	116	-0.1				

Cleveland Prospects

The State of the System:
Like their cross-state National League rivals, this is a very deep system that may lack true impact talent at the top. Well, at least at press time. One suspects it will get deeper and more impactful this offseason.

The Top Ten:

★ ★ ★ *2021 Top 101 Prospect* **#48** ★ ★ ★

1
George Valera CF   OFP: 60   ETA: 2023
Born: 11/13/00   Age: 20   Bats: L   Throws: L   Height: 5'11"   Weight: 185
Origin: International Free Agent, 2017

The Report: Valera's swing is not what you would call traditionally beautiful. And the bar for a pretty lefty swing is high anyway. But it's attractive in the same way a Seijun Suzuki film is—noisy, chaotic, frenetic while just barely under control, and probably best enjoyed in cinemascope. It's also short and to the point once it gets going, and often ends in an explosion of monochromatic violence. There's near-elite bat speed, and the raw power has become the party piece here—he was trending power-over-hit in the Penn League in 2019—although we still expect him to hit for a high enough average as well. He's likely bound for a corner eventually, but the bat should play there.

Development Track: Valera is one of the prospects I'm most personally annoyed didn't get a full 2020 season to crush A-ball. It would make ranking him number one in the Cleveland system far easier. The alternate site and instructional league reports don't give us any reason to move off our aggressive 2019 ranking, but we'd like to see it in games in 2021.

Variance: Extreme. Valera hasn't actually played in full-season ball yet and may end up in an outfield corner. There's significant pressure on the bat to play to projection.

Mark Barry's Fantasy Take: On one hand, all of the reasons to love Valera are still there—excellent bat speed, raw power, budding hit tool. On the other, he didn't play any real games in 2020, and because fantasy managers are nothing if not a fickle, prisoners of the moment, that's likely to cause his value to take a serious hit. Put those hands together and you have a buy-low opportunity on a dude who could be .290ish with 25-30 homers.

Cleveland 2021

★ ★ ★ 2021 Top 101 Prospect #52 ★ ★ ★

2 Nolan Jones 3B   OFP: 60   ETA: Late 2021/Early 2022
Born: 05/07/98   Age: 23   Bats: L   Throws: R   Height: 6'2"   Weight: 185
Origin: Round 2, 2016 Draft (#55 overall)

The Report: Jones was a cold weather prep shortstop who was going to quickly move off shortstop, but had the bat to carry a corner. So far...mostly so good. The raw power jumped quickly as Jones filled out in his late teens and is now plus-plus, although he's never slugged .500 at any minor league stop. The main culprit there is significant swing-and-miss to his game, with the K-rate peaking over 30 percent in his first taste of Double-A in 2019. He sometimes tries to yank it 450 feet, leading to whiffs when he can't adjust, although his overall approach is solid enough. If this sounds like a TTO slugger, well that's the outcome you are hoping for. Jones is passable at third base for now, but the arm and foot speed outpace the hands and lateral range, so he might be a better fit in right field. That might be more useful given Cleveland's current roster holes anyway.

Development Track: Jones spent the summer at the alternate site in Lake County, but really could have used another crack at the Eastern League to smooth out some of the rough edges of the offensive profile. Now you could argue that for him—and any number of other prospects we'll chronicle on these lists—seeing Triston McKenzie, Sam Hentges, and Nick Sandlin would be at least a comparable level of difficulty, but I'm not sure the instructional league type format is allowing for the kind of hit tool development Jones needs. I'm not sure that it isn't either. We'll see in April ... hopefully.

Variance: High. The power is loud but more raw than game. There is significant swing-and-miss and positional risk in the eventual major-league profile.

Mark Barry's Fantasy Take: The fun part about Cleveland's big-league roster is that Jones could be the "best" outfielder on the team should he get the call. Sure that's damning with faint praise, but whatever. It was probably telling that Jones didn't see any time with the big club in a season where top-75 prospects were being called up on a seemingly daily basis, but like Jeffrey said above, he still could use a little time to sand down the swing-and-miss in his profile. I don't love TTO prospects for fantasy (unless you're in an OBP league), so I'm less than enthused with Jones's upside.

★ ★ ★ 2021 Top 101 Prospect #73 ★ ★ ★

3 Triston McKenzie RHP   OFP: 60   ETA: Debuted in 2020
Born: 08/02/97   Age: 23   Bats: R   Throws: R   Height: 6'5"   Weight: 165
Origin: Round 1, 2015 Draft (#42 overall)

The Report: McKenzie was a former Top 101 prospect who dropped off Cleveland's top 10 last year because ... well, he didn't pitch. After missing time in 2018 with a forearm strain, back issues wiped out his 2019. He was reportedly having a normal spring, but given his rather narrow physique, you'd be forgiven for having concerns about whether he'd come back and be able to handle a full starter's workload. The stuff was Top 101 quality two years ago, but we were still relying on a bit of fastball projection to get him to the mid-rotation OFP.

Development Track: I called McKenzie a "mystery box" right before his 2020 debut. But behind Door #1, you got a pitcher pumping 95 with the same above-average 12-6 downer curve. There was also a new slider he had some feel for, and while his change was firm, McKenzie sold it well enough with his arm action to be effective. In a season of impressive pitching prospect debuts, he might have had the most dominant first outing. But the velocity went backward quickly after that first start and he was more 90-92 by his last few abbreviated September outings. He can still be effective in that velocity band given the deception, life, and command on the fastball. McKenzie hadn't thrown in games for almost two years before he was dropped into Cleveland's rotation, so it's not a huge surprise the velocity backslid some, but he also never really sat 95 in the minors either, so it's unclear what to expect here going forward. He does remain remarkably thin, and the physical projection we hoped for out of the draft doesn't seem to be coming.

Variance: High. This all depends on where the fastball/stamina settle after a normal (hopefully healthy) offseason and spring. He can be a useful major league starter in the low 90s, but the role 6 guy probably needs above-average fastball velocity for the rest of the arsenal to play off of. McKenzie also has a bad injury track record, so there will be durability questions until he takes the ball every fifth day while maintaining the stuff and command.

Mark Barry's Fantasy Take: It's hard to call McKenzie's debut anything other than an huge success after spending the better part of two seasons on the sidelines. Where that leaves us, though, uh, your guess is as good as mine. He's probably an SP4 factoring in all of the risk, but I'd be surprised if he's not valued a little better than that on the market. I'm a big fan of the dude and the story, but the variance is high.

─────── ★ ★ ★ *2021 Top 101 Prospect* **#87** ★ ★ ★ ───────

4 **Gabriel Arias** **SS**   OFP: 60   ETA: 2022
Born: 02/27/00   Age: 21   Bats: R   Throws: R   Height: 6'1"   Weight: 201
Origin: International Free Agent, 2016

The Report: Arias's 2019 offensive improvements were hidden some by a rough first half. After July 1st, the 19-year-old slashed .350/.378/.562, smashing 10 of his 17 High-A home runs. It wasn't random small sample size success either, as multiple looks by our staff saw improvements at the plate as the season wore on. While he's unlikely to hit .300 with pop outside of the friendly confines of Lake

Elsinore, both his hit and power tools could land at a tick above-average if he continues to further refine an aggressive approach. Even if they don't, the plus shortstop glove should carry the profile at least to a useful fifth infielder.

Development Track: Arias was the main prospect piece sent to Cleveland at the deadline for Mike Clevinger. He may soon enough be putting down his marker as a potential Lindor replacement at the 6. Arias isn't major-league-ready on the whole—although the glove might be—but if you are willing to wait another year, and the bat proves to be above-average, you might end up with merely a Betts-to-Verdugo type downgrade there. I guess here's hopin' if you are a Cleveland fan?

Variance: High. The glove gives Arias a soft landing on a major league bench even if the offensive improvements of 2019 prove to be a Cal League mirage. In that respect, really wish we had another year of improvement with the bat to point to.

Mark Barry's Fantasy Take: First of all, no. How dare you? No "here's hopin' as a Cleveland fan."

Having said that, I do like Arias and don't be fooled by the Josh Naylor-of-it-all, Arias was likely the crown jewel of the Clevinger trade. In the Golden Age of the Fantasy Shortstop, Arias will need to run some to have seasons where he cracks into the Top 10 at the position, but presently gives me 2020 Dansby Swanson-vibes if he continues this trajectory.

───────── ★ ★ ★ *2021 Top 101 Prospect* **#100** ★ ★ ★ ─────────

5 **Daniel Espino** **RHP** OFP: 60 ETA: 2023
Born: 01/05/01 Age: 20 Bats: R Throws: R Height: 6'2" Weight: 205
Origin: Round 1, 2019 Draft (#24 overall)

The Report: A lightning rod in the 2019 draft, Espino was considered to have the type of arm talent usually associated with a top-10 pick. Enough teams worried about the length in his arm action to question his long-term health projection, causing him to "slip" to the 23rd pick overall. The fastball is lively—routinely in the mid-90s and nearing 100 in shorter outings—and he has surprisingly good command for a young player throwing that kind of fuzz. Additionally, there are the makings of two plus breaking balls, both of which he is unafraid of throwing to righties and lefties alike. The consensus has always been that his premium athleticism on the mound should allow for any necessary adjustments to be integrated seamlessly as he develops into a potential dynamic starter.

Development Track: Despite his age and limited pro experience, Espino was able to get much-needed repetitions this summer and fall at their team's alternate site and training camps. Even after the long spring layoff, his velocity held at previous norms while continuing his path towards throwing high quality strikes. Likened to a "ball of clay," he is being molded by a player development group that has shown a nearly unmatched track record of bettering in-house prospects into eventual major league difference-makers on the mound.

Variance: High. Some of the concerns that plagued his pre-draft report still exist even though they have yet to manifest negatively. As time goes on with the continued reps those worries will dissipate more fully. If everything goes right, he could be a star.

Mark Barry's Fantasy Take: Espino is one of my favorite non-marquee pitching prospects. He's got the velocity, the pitch mix, and the ability to strike tons of dudes out to be a front-line starter. What could possibly go wrong (dammit, oops sorry trying to delete—baseball gods don't read this)?

6   Brayan Rocchio   SS   OFP: 55   ETA: 2023/24
Born: 01/13/01   Age: 20   Bats: S   Throws: R   Height: 5'10"   Weight: 150
Origin: International Free Agent, 2017

The Report: Bursting out of the gates in his professional debut, despite a modest six-figure signing bonus, the combined offensive and defensive abilities for Rocchio were noticeable from day one. Most notable is his contact rate from both sides of the plate, while appearing more comfortable from the left side, his right-handed swing isn't far behind. His featherweight size won't likely allow for much growth in the power department, but a plus hit tool with plus grades defensively at either shortstop or second base translate to a future starter role.

Development Track: Like many Venezuelans during the pandemic, travel restrictions hampered his ability to make it into the United States for additional training. Cleveland was able to set up online training sessions with many of their international prospects, where Rocchio received glowing reviews for his diligence and information retention while working out on a neighborhood diamond. Strength training is at the top of his list for needed development, followed by the need to face more advanced pitching to test the bat.

Variance: Extreme. Rocchio is the type of player most negatively affected from the lost year. The bat could be special, but it might also be much ado about nothing.

Mark Barry's Fantasy Take: There's a wide range of outcomes for Rocchio right now, as Keanan correctly points out that it is indeed difficult to learn baseball on a Zoom call. His potential is a lot of fun, maybe a little Cesar Hernandez-esque from a fantasy production standpoint, but the mystery of his 2020 development makes it risky to dive in headfirst.

7   Ethan Hankins   RHP   OFP: 55   ETA: 2023
Born: 05/23/00   Age: 21   Bats: R   Throws: R   Height: 6'6"   Weight: 200
Origin: Round 1, 2018 Draft (#35 overall)

The Report: During the summer showcase season of 2017, Hankins elevated himself to the top spot of the prep arm pecking order due to the sheer movement on his pitches paired with a 6-foot-6 workhorse frame. There was concern that his delivery lacked consistency, at times showing wide variance between starts. When spring 2018 rolled around, Hankins dealt with shoulder soreness, further exacerbating questions about the delivery and the long-term prognosis on his throwing arm. His mechanics have since been simplified, especially in the bottom half, while maintaining the plus movement on his mid-90s fastball. With the revamped delivery he has lost some break to the slider, while the changeup has the potential to be his best secondary pitch when all is said and done.

Development Track: Like his teammate Espino, Hankins got the reps he desperately needed this year. With a focus on strike-throwing and staying within himself, he made positive strides especially in Cleveland's fall camp. Even though there is some risk of an eventual reliever role, he certainly improved his likelihood to stick in the rotation after his 2020 progress. He'll be given every opportunity to start so long as his mechanics continue trending in the right direction and his secondary pitches catch up to his fastball quality.

Variance: High. The building blocks exist to be a full-time starter even though the trajectory so far might not indicate it's likely.

Mark Barry's Fantasy Take: Injury concerns aside (lol), there are worse organizations to bet on when developing young, talented arms. The laws of TINSTAAPP apply, as always, but if you're rostering hurlers who have yet to see High-A, Hankins is the kind of guy I'd like to gamble on, especially in that top-125ish range.

8. Tyler Freeman SS   OFP: 55   ETA: 2022
Born: 05/21/99   Age: 22   Bats: R   Throws: R   Height: 6'0"   Weight: 170
Origin: Round 2, 2017 Draft (#71 overall)

The Report: I don't mean to step on Mark's toes here, but Freeman is the quintessential "better fantasy prospect than real life one" for me. He's not a bad prospect by any means. Despite a rather mechanical and at times overly-complicated stroke, he makes consistent good contact and you can project a plus hit tool. Freeman is also a plus runner and an efficient base-stealer, so you get batting average and steals from a player who is also likely to have some positional flexibility—that is to say, he's unlikely to have enough glove to be a full-time shortstop. There isn't going to be much in the way of power or OBP to boost the overall offensive profile, so he profiles best as a batting average driven second baseman.

Development Track: The reports from the alternate site don't really move the needle a ton, but he moves up some on attrition elsewhere in the system and the rest on my waning stubbornness about the profile. Still would like to see that swing against better velocity and secondaries in Double-A first, though.

Variance: High. Hit is the carrying tool here and we haven't seen Freeman rake against upper minors pitchers yet.

Mark Barry's Fantasy Take: Yep, I concur. Freeman is a borderline top-50 dynasty prospect for me, and if any semblance of power comes, he could rise a good deal higher than that.

9 Aaron Bracho   SS   OFP: 55   ETA: 2023
Born: 04/24/01   Age: 20   Bats: S   Throws: R   Height: 5'11"   Weight: 175
Origin: International Free Agent, 2017

The Report: Not unlike his Venezuelan teammate Rocchio, Bracho is a bat-first infielder. The similarities, however, tail off significantly after that. Bracho's body is physically filled out with little projection left even though he won't turn 20 until the presumptive minor league season starts in 2021. It's not that he's round or unathletic, it's more of a ready-made boxy frame that isn't likely to change much. He's only played second base as a professional, yet there are questions as to whether he'd fare better hidden in the outfield. In order for that to happen, the bat needs to carry him into the lineup—which it does in spades. He controls the zone well, squaring fastballs up and fighting off breaking balls consistently to run long counts and get on base. He's adept from both sides of the plate as a switch hitter, and like so many of his organizational teammates, there is a lot to dream on.

Development Track: Injuries delayed his pro debut by over a year, getting only 38 games under his belt in 2019. To make up for lost time, he was given a coveted spot on the 60-man alternate site roster where he competed well against players much more advanced in their careers. Using that experience, he will be one to watch next season as someone who could take several steps forward.

Variance: High. The juxtaposition against the myriad other infielder prospects within the org has Bracho with a higher offensive potential without the backup plan that others might have.

Mark Barry's Fantasy Take: Oh look, another high-contact, middle infielder who gets on base. If I didn't know any better, I'd think these guys grow on trees, but I know we don't have the technology for something like that yet. Anyway, Bracho has a chance to hit a lot, even if his defensive position might ultimately be TBD. He's a fringy top-100 fantasy guy right now, even if he's not a game changer anywhere.

10 Carson Tucker   SS   OFP: 50   ETA: 2025
Born: 01/24/02   Age: 19   Bats: R   Throws: R   Height: 6'2"   Weight: 180
Origin: Round 1, 2020 Draft (#23 overall)

The Report: Carson is Pirates shortstop Cole Tucker's younger brother, and it was a bit of a surprise when he was popped in the first round of the draft. Lacking any flashy tools, he is more of a high-floor type and signed an under-slot deal as Cleveland chose to employ a spread-the-bonus-pool strategy. Tucker is still growing into his body—as evidenced by a two-inch growth spurt his senior year—and working to find a swing he's comfortable with. At present he shows very good foot speed and the defensive chops to stick at short.

Development Track: As his draft year went along, there were some positive signs in the swing that likely helped cement his draft standing with the team. In the time it takes him to gain strength, especially in the lower half, he'll be able to find a better setup that helps begin the swing and engage the top half. His hands are a bit tighter with less movement, limiting all the moving parts that pre-existed throughout. First step: get into that pro strength program.

Variance: Extreme. Tucker is still growing and his swing is protean as a result, so he has a long way to go.

Mark Barry's Fantasy Take: Meh. Tucker could be good, but a lot of things need to happen for that to come to fruition. And even if it does, it's likely not terribly fantasy relevant. Toss Tucker on the watchlist if you'd like, but don't expect returns for a few years.

The Prospects You Meet Outside The Top Ten:

#11

Tanner Burns   RHP   Born: 12/28/98   Age: 22   Bats: R   Throws: R   Height: 6'0"   Weight: 215   Origin: Round 1, 2020 Draft (#36 overall)
An exceptional performer in the SEC over three seasons, Burns improved each year even as he continuously found success. A fastball-first pitcher, he can both cut and sink the pitch while hiding it well during his delivery. He establishes the heater in each quadrant early in the game before turning to his secondary pitches. The curveball is the best of the secondaries, however, the command of the rest of the arsenal lags behind that of his heater. The ceiling may not be as high, but he's likely to find a reliable back-end starter role.

MLB-ready arms, but probably relievers

Emmanuel Clase   RHP   Born: 03/18/98   Age: 23   Bats: R   Throws: R   Height: 6'2"   Weight: 206   Origin: International Free Agent, 2015
Acquired in the Corey Kluber trade last offseason, Clase had a completely lost season; he suffered a back injury early in spring training and then got popped for a steroid in May and was suspended for the entire shortened season. We'd heard in our canvassing of the system that he was back to full strength, and he looked as much in his first appearance in the Dominican Winter League a few weeks ago. At his best, Clase has one of the best weapons in baseball: a high-90s cutter—and it's a true cutter at that high of a speed, not a fastball with a little bit of natural cut—that regularly hits 100, which you probably saw a bunch of GIFs of in 2019.

He also has a plus slider, and generally the whole package is unhittable when he's healthy and throwing strikes. He should be a high-leverage reliever starting right now.

Prospects to dream on a little

Bo Naylor   C   Born: 02/21/00   Age: 21   Bats: L   Throws: R   Height: 6'0"   Weight: 195   Origin: Round 1, 2018 Draft (#29 overall)
Part of the second high-profile set of brothers in the org, the younger of the Naylor brothers is often unfairly compared to his older sibling Josh. While he has a similar squarish frame, his athleticism is much better and gives him a chance to stick behind the plate when paired with his close-to-average catch-and-throw ability. The calling card offensively is a power stroke that is easy-plus on the raw side and shows up plenty in games. Of course there are a lot of strikeouts to go with that, but he fits the mold of what is expected of today's archetypal catcher.

Lenny Torres   RHP   Born: 10/15/00   Age: 20   Bats: R   Throws: R   Height: 6'1"   Weight: 190   Origin: Round 1, 2018 Draft (#41 overall)
One of the youngest players in the 2018 draft class, Torres fit Cleveland's trend of valuing age with its corollary of physical projection. His pro debut in the AZL was very loud, as he showed an athletic delivery with a plus heater, makings of a plus slider, and feel for a change. Unfortunately, the following spring he underwent Tommy John surgery and missed all of 2019. The rehab process during 2020 would have been very cautious regardless, so you can expect Torres to hit the ground running in 2021, especially after adding lean muscle to his frame during the time off from game action.

The New Guys

Joey Cantillo   LHP   Born: 12/18/99   Age: 21   Bats: L   Throws: L   Height: 6'4"   Weight: 220   Origin: Round 16, 2017 Draft (#468 overall)
Every season there's a few A-ball pitchers who absolutely dominate the level with an advanced changeup and an upper-80s fastball they can move around the zone. Cantillo was far younger than the median of that group—he spent 2019 as still a teenager—and may still add a tick or two, but overall the stats far outpaced the stuff. You could certainly argue Cleveland is the right place for him to add enough velocity and a suddenly viable slide/cutter thing. It wouldn't be the first time. But until we see signs of that, we can't bake it into his projection.

Owen Miller   SS   Born: 11/15/96   Age: 24   Bats: R   Throws: R   Height: 5'11"   Weight: 197   Origin: Round 3, 2018 Draft (#84 overall)

Cantillo had the eye-popping numbers in 2019, but we ranked Miller as the better prospect on the 2020 Padres list. He's broadly similar to Tyler Freeman, with a bit more pop, but more likely to end up as a utility type than an everyday middle infielder. But this ranking—or lack thereof—overstates the gap between them as prospects.

Safe MLB bats, but less upside than you'd like

Daniel Johnson   RF   Born: 07/11/95   Age: 25   Bats: L   Throws: L   Height: 5'10"   Weight: 200   Origin: Round 5, 2016 Draft (#154 overall)

Johnson got a brief look in the bigs in 2020, where he continued to try and swing very, very hard at major league stuff. He has a plus power/speed combo, and the arm is even better than that, but until he reins in his aggressive, leveraged stroke, he'll struggle to establish himself as more than an optionable 26th man.

Top Talents 25 and Under (as of 4/1/2021):

1. Shane Bieber, RHP
2. George Valera, OF
3. Nolan Jones, 3B
4. James Karinchak, RHP
5. Triston McKenzie, RHP
6. Franmil Reyes, DH/OF
7. Gabriel Arias, SS
8. Daniel Espino, RHP
9. Brayan Rocchio, SS
10. Ethan Hankins, RHP

Shane Bieber, the reigning American League Cy Young Award winner, has developed into one of the very best pitchers in baseball. I've written previously on how even merely solid prospects have a 99th-percentile outcome of a superstar; that's Bieber's present trajectory.

James Karinchak, our 2020 No. 101 prospect, lived up to his billing and finished sixth in Rookie of the Year balloting. He trotted in from the bullpen with Wild Thing blaring over the speakers, stomped around the mound like a maniac, threw a bunch of 70-to-80-grade fastballs and curveballs, walked just a few too many for comfort, and struck out 53 of the 109 batters he faced. It was everything we'd hoped for, and just about the only real negative was that his velocity was a little down at times, not that it made his fastball less effective. Karinchak seems poised to take over the closer's role as soon as this year, and should continue to be one of the more entertaining and dominant relievers for the foreseeable future.

Franmil Reyes is generously listed with a secondary position in the outfield, which is sort of true in that he can stand there if you really want him to for some reason. He started 58 games in 2020 and 57 of them were at DH, matching his poor defensive reputation. Reyes has light-tower power and crushes the ball when he hits it, posting exit velocities near the top of the league. His overall offensive performance has been more above-average than star-level so far, and DH carries a high enough offensive burden that he could stand to inch that production up.

With a deep farm system—the top eight prospects in the system are all viable Top 101 candidates—only those three non-prospect eligible players made the 25 and under list. But that obscures the strength of Cleveland's young major-league talent a bit. In a weaker system, Aaron Civale, Josh Naylor, Jake Bauers, Logan Allen, and Yu Chang all might've made this list.

Part 3: Featured Articles

Cleveland All-Time Top 10 Players

by Matthew Trueblood

POSITION PLAYERS

JIM THOME, 1B/3B (1991–2002, 2011)
The most impressive thing about Thome is that no one ever had to explain to him (and he never had to work to figure out for himself) that it was worth working deep counts and not sweating strikeouts in order to maximize power. Given his skill set, the more plate appearances he could force to one of the three true outcomes, the better, and from the very start he did that brilliantly. During his eight full seasons with Cleveland, he used his vicious, low-swooping uppercut to post a 1.004 OPS. Over 48 percent of his trips to the plate ended in walks, whiffs, or homers.

NAP LAJOIE, 2B (1902–1914)
In hindsight, maybe Cleveland should have just kept the nickname they adopted when they acquired (and shortly after made a player-manager of) Lajoie in the earliest days of the American League: the Cleveland Naps. To brand an entire team around a single player seems anathema to the game as we now understand it, but Lajoie was the first true superstar of the entire AL, so it seemed natural. He had tremendous power for the Dead Ball Era, revolutionized infield defense, and stood out as one of the biggest players in the game. He's best remembered for hitting .426 in the AL's inaugural season, but some of his later seasons, such as 1904 (.376/.413/.546) and 1910 (.383/.444/.514) were just as good and took place in a league that had increased its level of competition over time.

TERRY TURNER, SS/3 (1904–1918)
Famous for his head-first slides, Turner was a defensive whiz, and proved better able to keep providing value with his glove than most players could. In his early and mid-20s, he was arguably the best defensive shortstop in the American

League. Thereafter, he flitted between second and third base, but continued to be great at each position. He remains Cleveland's all-time leader in games played, edging Lajoie by five games. The only player of recent vintage on the list is Omar Vizauel, 10th with 1,478. All the others have long since gone on to Valhalla. This may say something more about the vagaries of the Cleveland franchise over the years than it does about Turner's greatness.

JOE SEWELL, SS (1920–1930)

With his famous, humongous, never-broken bat, Sewell put on the best long-running display of contact skills in baseball history. From 1925 through his final season in 1933, he averaged 616 plate appearances per season—and five strikeouts. What we know about the dramatic differences between today's game and the one Sewell played might tempt us to think of this as merely impressive; it's much more than that. Even by the standards of his time, Sewell was a wizard. Even the timing of his emergence was magical—he was promoted to replace the great Ray Chapman after the latter's fatal beaning on August 16, 1920. His immediate excellence at bat helped the team come out on top in a tight pennant race and go on to win the World Series. His .320 career average remains in the top 10 in team history.

LOU BOUDREAU, SS (1938–1950)

In a radical stroke that spoke both to Boudreau's baseball perspicacity and the team's penchant for marketing stunts, Boudreau was named player-manager for the 1942 season, at age 24. He would remain in that role until he left for Boston in 1951, meaning that he was not only the best player on the last Cleveland team to win the World Series and the league MVP that year to boot, but the manager of it. Boudreau the player made Boudreau the manager look good: his .355/.453/.534 season remains one of the best a shortstop has ever had. Despite a lack of speed, he was a phenomenal defensive shortstop, holding onto that skill even into his 30s, and a great contact hitter. As skipper, he popularized the Ted Williams shift.

TRIS SPEAKER, OF (1916–1926)

That Sad Sam Jones went on to have a fine career and the Red Sox did manage another championship after trading Speaker to Cleveland shouldn't stop us from thinking of the Speaker deal as an equal partner to the sale of Babe Ruth in Boston's decades of frustration thereafter (or the Mookie Betts trade 100 years after that). Though there were character issues in play with both Tris and the Babe, the motive in all three cases was largely financianl.Speaker had a Frank Robinson-like reaction to being traded in his prime, winning the rate-stat Triple Crown (.386/.470/.502) in his first year with Cleveland. Taking over as manager, he also led the team to the 1920 championship. Until Willie Mays came along, he was considered the best defensive center fielder ever. He holds the all-time record for doubles (792), which is unlikely to be broken anytime in the next 50 years.

SHOELESS JOE JACKSON, OF (1910–1915)
His ignominious end in pro baseball has tied Jackson's legacy to the White Sox, but he had his best seasons in Cleveland. He hit .408 in 1911, led the league in total bases in 1912, and posted the highest OPS in baseball in 1913. Though they got two credible players in exchange, the team's decision to trade Jackson to Chicago was primarily about the $50,000 they eventually got, and as such, it might be the most scandalous monetary transaction related to Jackson's baseball career.

EARL AVERILL, OF (1929–1939)
Averill was a solid defensive center fielder and a dangerous left-handed slugger, at a time when center fielders didn't hit for power. Ty Cobb and Speaker retired in 1929, the year before Averill debuted. He was in his mid-30s when Joe DiMaggio came up in 1936. In the years between, Averill's career ISO of .216 tops his nearest competitor (Earle Combs) by roughly 80 points. Averill was only 5-foot-9, and when he first reported Cleveland owner Alva Bradley complained to general manager Billy Evans, "You paid all that money for a midget." But baseball allows success by many physical types and like his contemporary Hack Wilson, Averill was small but strong. Because he'd spent three years in the Pacific Coast League and was purchased by Cleveland when he was 27, Averill had a shorter career than most great players, and he was in his mid-70s when the Veterans Committee elected him to the Hall of Fame. That's a reflection with voters' obsession with counting stats rather than of Averill's quality—he was very good.

LARRY DOBY, OF (1947-1955, 1958)
Far too little respect and admiration accrues to Doby. Given the partition between the leagues at that time, Dobby was in no sense less of a pioneer than Jackie Robinson. In Detroit, Washington, D.C., and Cleveland itself, he was the first Black man to take the field in the modern major leagues. He faced racism and abuse not at all dissimilar to what Robinson received, at a much younger age, and with less careful preparation. Despite that, he was a great player. He struck out at rates fans and teams were not inclined to forgive at the time, but he got great power, a high batting average on balls in play, and plenty of walks in the bargain. He also played solid defense in center field.

KENNY LOFTON, OF (1992–2001, 2007)
He was too good an athlete to have his best possible baseball career; playing basketball at the University of Arizona slowed his entry into pro ball. A Lou Brock-style speed demon who happened to break in just as baseball began a new

fixation on power, Lofton was often underappreciated, as first evidenced by the trade that sent him from Houston to Cleveland (for catcher Eddie Taubensee and pitcher Willie Blair) before he had even exhausted his rookie status. He should have won the American League MVP award in 1994 but was only a peripheral consideration for it. In each of his first five seasons, he led the AL in steals, and although his baserunning pace slowed thereafter, he continued to hit. The Brock comparison is almost fair, but Lofton walked more and was a consistently excellent defensive center fielder as opposed to a middling left fielder. Eventually, he'll join Brock in Cooperstown, wearing a Cleveland cap.

PITCHERS

ADDIE JOSS, RHP (1902–1910)

Owner of the lowest WHIP in baseball history, Joss comes by that honor in a tragic way. He died just after Opening Day, 1911 due to tubercular meningitis, which had probably also accounted for some previous creeping health problems. Before that, he was one of the best pitchers in baseball for his entire career. He used a corkscrew delivery, showing batters his back, then fired over-the-top fastballs and curves. Despite the unusual windup, he had excellent control, which made him extremely tough to handle and his career ERA of 1.89 is not solely a product of his era.

STAN COVELESKI, RHP (1916–1924)

One of the most famous purveyors of the spitball, Coveleski was grandfathered in when that pitch was outlawed in 1921. Often, the spitter was a pitch akin to the knuckleball in that even its most ardent users struggled to control it. Not so with Coveleski, who used wrist action to manipulate the pitch and could give it two-plane break. He was known as especially reliant on the spitball, but he could probably have thrived with a dry breaking ball if he'd needed to. As it was, he was an excellent workhorse in nine seasons with Cleveland and was the pitching hero of their 1920 World Series win. Traded to the defending champion Senators after an off year; Covleski and the team had grown disenchanted with each other. He rebounded to 20-5 with a league-leading 2.84 ERA. The return, Carr Smith and By Speece, wasn't that good.

WILLIS HUDLIN, RHP (1926–1940)

Hudlin was only an average starter, but he maintained that level for almost 15 seasons for Cleveland. He didn't have an especially good second pitch, technically speaking, but he mixed things up by sometimes throwing his fastball straight over the top with riding action, and sometimes switching to sidearm, achieving great sinking action. That his arm held up as long as it did, given that style, is impressive, even if he never had even a sustained period of real dominance. A baseball lifer, he continued to coach, manage, and scout for decades after the end of his pitching career.

MEL HARDER, RHP (1928–1947)

Called up at an exceptionally young age, Harder had nothing but a power sinker for his first few years. He eventually built a good repertoire around that, though, including an impressive curveball. From 1932-35, he was great, sailing along at an average of over 250 innings per year and shredding the league, but in late July 1936, he hurt his arm badly. Remarkably, he kept pitching, but in his final 13 appearances that year, he had an 8.44 ERA and batters hit .377 against him. He was never the same, but became a modestly effective junkballer and hung around long enough to teach Bob Lemon the slider.

BOB FELLER, RHP (1936–1941 1945–1956)

Stories about Feller—not even the legendary ones, but the true, documented facts of his career—verge on unbelievable. He threw so hard that he inspired bizarrely excited attempts to measure his speed, including having his fastball racing a speeding motorcycle. He debuted at 17 and never did pitch in the minor leagues. He enlisted the day after the bombing of Pearl Harbor and did not come home to baseball until the war was over. He also led the majors in strikeouts seven times, and in wins five times, but also once walked 208 batters in a season. He ran so Nolan Ryan could fly. ?/p>

BOB LEMON, RHP (1941–1942, 1946–1958)

Converted from third base, Lemon hit 37 home runs in his career and averaged .282/.310/.418 with two homers as a pinch-hitter. That was just the icing on the cake: By wide acclaim, Lemon had one of the best sliders ever, and certainly an elite one for his time and place. He also had one of the better sinkers of all time. Notably presaging the way we now think of pitching, Lemon once said that he had no true fastball because he considered the sinker (his moved a lot, especially to the arm side) distinct from a traditional heater. Lemon's goal was never to throw anything straight, and using that approach, he was one of the most durable and deepest-working starters in the game for a decade.

MIKE GARCÍA, RHP (1948–1959)

As a rookie in 1949, García led the majors in ERA and the AL in FIP and strikeout-to-walk ratio, all while serving as a swingman who started just half the games in which he appeared. He would win three more FIP crowns, though no one gave those out back then, largely by having one of the best fastballs in the big leagues and good control thereof. Nicknamed "Big Bear," he had that kind of ursine presence on the mound, despite not being physically massive. He had a languid delivery, which only made the heat seem hotter once it got moving.

With an arrival delayed by service in World War II and a workload that built to a crushing 292.1 innings (1952) despite his swingman status his peak didn't last long, but he had time for a second ERA title in 1954.

EARLY WYNN, RHP (1949–1957, 1963)

Wynn is another case of Harder's mentorship paying off. He taught Wynn better versions of the curveball and slider and helped him develop confidence in his changeup. Wynn would always walk many hitters, but as he learned to pitch with a deep repertoire, he started piling up strikeouts, too; before coming to Cleveland his career strikeout rate was 2.7 per nine. It was 5.3 per nine thereafter. He had started using tunneling to attack the top of the strike zone, in violation of conventional wisdom at the time. Returned to Cleveland to pick up his 300th and last win after five years with the White Sox.

SAM MCDOWELL, LHP (1961–1971)

Throwing hard is the surest foundation for strikeout success, and the surest way to earn the nickname "Sudden" Sam. McDowell threw hard, and although he didn't always know where his stuff was going, he won five strikeout crowns. He was huge and left-handed, and thus drew unfair comparisons to Sandy Koufax early in his career. That led to some sense of disappointment in what was really a great career in which he led the American League in strikeout rate in six different seasons. Like Koufax, he ran into arm trouble by his mid-20s, and was of little use after age 30. McDowell is sometimes better remembered for his candid discussion of his alcoholism and his subsequent turn to counseling others suffering from the same affliction. It's an important and moving story, but he was a great pitcher too.

COREY KLUBER, RHP (2011–2019)

A throw-in of a trade acquisition after being an afterthought of a draftee by the Padres, the goal of which was to get outfielder Ryan Ludwick to San Diego, Kluber became a two-time Cy Young Award-winner with such efficiency and poise that he was nicknamed "Klubot". He could throw a power sinker with deadly precision and a cutter that would veer the opposite way and located both well to each side of home plate. He had two plus breaking balls. From 2014 through 2018, he pitched almost 1,100 innings, had a DRA- of 65, and was worth 30.7 WARP. He carried Cleveland through the 2016 postseason to Game 7 of the World Series where, clearly exhausted, he finally ran out of gas. Despite a short career (so far), he's a future Hall of Famer.

A Taxonomy of 2020 Abnormalities

by Rob Mains

I'm going to start this with a trivia question. Trust me, it's relevant. Don't bother skipping to the end of the article to find the answer, it's not there.

Only five players have appeared in 140 or more games for 16 straight seasons. Who are they?

It's a trivia question starting off an essay, so you know how this works: Whatever you guessed, you're wrong. It's okay. As someone who purchased this book, chances are good that you're an educated baseball fan. But the circumstances behind 2020 force us to abandon, or at least seriously question, some of our favorite patterns and crutches for evaluating the game we love.

We just completed what was undoubtedly the strangest season in MLB history. No fans, geographically limited schedule, universal DH, seven-inning twin bills, runners on second in extra innings, a 16-team postseason, a club playing at a Triple-A stadium. Some of these changes will likely persist (sorry), but we've never had so many tweaks dumped on us all at once, at least not since they figured out how many balls were in a walk.

And the biggest, of course, was the 60-game season. The 19th century was dotted with teams that went bankrupt before the season ended, but the lone season with only 60 scheduled games was 1877. That year there were only six teams, the league rostered a total of 77 players (just 16 more than the 2020 Marlins), and batters called for pitches to be thrown high or low by the pitcher, who was 50 feet away. We can say the 2020 season was easily the shortest ever for recognizable baseball.

As such, it'll stand out. Few abbreviated seasons do. Just about everybody reading this knows the 1994 season ended after Seattle's Randy Johnson struck out Oakland's Ernie Young for the last out of the Mariners-A's game on August 11. The ensuing player strike wiped out the rest of the season and the postseason. Teams played only 112-117 games that year.

And many of you know that a strike in the middle of the 1981 season split the season in two, resulting in the only Division Series until 1995. Teams played only 103-111 games that year, the shortest regular season since 1885.

Those two seasons are memorable. So when we see that nobody drove in 100 runs in 1981, or that Greg Maddux was the only pitcher with 180 or more innings pitched in 1994, we think, "Of course. Strike year."

But we don't remember other short years. You might not recall that the 1994 strike spilled into the next year, chopping 18 games off the 1995 schedule. You might've read that the 1918 season, played during the last pandemic, ended after Labor Day due to the government's World War I "work or fight" order. A strike erased the first week and a half of the 1972 season, but that year's best known as the last time pitchers batted in the American League.

The point is, while we don't remember small changes to the schedule, we remember the big ones. The 1981 mid-season strike. The 1994 season- and Series-ending strike. And, of course, the pandemic-shortened 2020 season. We won't need a reminder why Marcell Ozuna's 18 homers were the fewest to lead the National League in a century. (Literally; Cy Williams led with 15 in 1920.)

Now, about that trivia question. The five players are Hank Aaron, Brooks Robinson, Pete Rose, Ichiro Suzuki, and Johnny Damon. The one nobody gets, of course, is Damon, and a lot of people miss Ichiro, whose last season of 140-plus games came garbed in the red-orange and ocean blue of Miami when he was 42. That's half of what makes it a good question. The other half is the two guys whom many think made the list but didn't. Lou Gehrig? His streak started in the Yankees' 42nd game of the 1925 season and lasted only 13 seasons after that. And everybody assumes Cal Ripken Jr. did it, having played 2,632 straight games over 17 seasons. But one of those 17 seasons was 1994, when the Orioles played only 112 games.

My point? *I just told you* everybody remembers the 1994 strike year, but everybody forgets it fell in the middle of Ripken's streak, separating the first twelve years from the last four. Just because we recall something doesn't mean it's always at the front of our minds.

Nobody is going to forget 2020, and baseball is obviously not the main reason. But there will come a time in the future when you're looking at a player's or a team's record, and there will be baffling numbers there for 2020, and you'll think, "I wonder what happened." (Not to mention the missing line for minor league players.) Just like you forgot that the 1994 strike limited Ripken to 112 games.

Try not to forget it, though. The 2020 season resulted in weird statistical results for several reasons.

There were only 60 games.
I know, duh. But that had impacts beyond counting stats like Ozuna's home run total or Yu Darvish and Shane Bieber leading the majors with eight wins. (I know, pitcher wins, but still.)

The 162-game season is the longest among major North American sports, and that duration gives us a gift. Over the course of a long season, small variations tend to even out. A player who has a ten-game hot streak will probably have a ten-game cold streak. A team that starts the year losing a bunch of close games will probably win a bunch of them. We get regression to the mean. Statistics stabilize.

Consider flipping a coin. Over the long run, we expect it to come up heads about half the time. But the fewer flips, the more variation there'll be. If you flip a coin six times, probability theory tells us you'll get at least two-third heads about 34 percent of the time. Flip it 30 times, your chance of two-thirds heads drops to five percent.

Or, relevant to this case, if you flip a coin 60 times, your chance of getting at least 36 heads—that's 60 percent—is 7.75 percent. Expand the coin-flipping to 162 times, and the chance of getting 60 percent heads drops to 0.73 percent.

In other words, the odds of an outcome that's 20 percent better (or worse) than expected is *more than ten times higher* when you flip your coin 60 times than when you do it 162 times. Call it small sample size, call lack of mean reversion, or call it luck not evening out, 162 is a lot more predictive than 60. You get much more variation over 60 games than over 162. Bieber's 1.63 ERA and 0.87 FIP aren't something we'd see over a full season, and neither is Javier Baéz's .203/.238/.360.

Some players' lines in 2020 look normal. Brian Anderson had an .811 OPS in 2019 and an .810 OPS in 2020. (He probably would have gotten that last point if he'd been given enough time.) But there are many like Bieber and Baéz, some of them from young players still establishing their talent levels. The answer to the question, "What went right or wrong for that guy in 2020?" is most likely "Nothing, it was just a 2020 thing."

Preseason training was abbreviated for hitters.
Every year, spring training drags. Players get tired of it, fans get tired of it, and you sure can tell sportswriters get tired of it. Yes, something to get everyone into shape is necessary, but does it really have to drag on for over a month? Can't we shorten it?

The 2020 season answered in the negative, at least for hitters. Warren Spahn is credited with saying that hitting is timing and pitching is upsetting timing. It appears nobody had his timing down after the abbreviated July summer camp. Through August 9—18 games into the season—MLB batters were hitting .230/.311/.395 with a .275 BABIP. That BABIP, had it held, would have been the lowest since 1968, the Year of the Pitcher. In recent years it's hovered around .300.

It didn't hold. Play returned to more normal levels the rest of the year: .249/.325/.425 with a .297 BABIP starting August 10. But batters whose play concentrated in those first two weeks wound up with ugly lines. Andrew

Benintendi went on the injured list with a season-ending rib cage strain on August 11. His final line: .103/.314/.128 in 14 games. Franchy Cordero went on the IL with a hamate bone fracture on August 9 and a .154/.185/.231 line. Even though he came back strong in a late September return, it was too late to repair his full-season numbers.

Preseason training was abbreviated for pitchers.

Every year, spring training drags. Players get tired of it, fans get tired of it ... wait, I already said that. But the abbreviated preseason was tough on pitchers, too. As noted, they had the upper hand coming out of the gate. But then they lost that hand. And then their arms, too.

The 2020 season was spread over 67 days. During those 67 days, 237 pitchers hit the Injured List, compared to 135 in the first 67 days of 2019. A lot of those IL stints, though, were COVID-19-related. Still, over the first 67 days of the 2019 season, there were 72 pitchers on the IL with arm injuries. That figure jumped to 110 in 2020, a 53 percent increase.

There are a number of factors contributing to pitcher arm injuries, ranging from usage to velocity, but it appears that attenuated preseason training played a role. A lot of pitchers had super-short seasons due to arm woes. Corey Kluber, Roberto Osuna, and Shohei Ohtani combined for seven innings, none after August 8. All suffered arm injuries. We'll never know whether they'd have fared better with a longer preseason, but we can guess how they probably feel.

Everybody played.

Rosters were set to expand from 25 to 26 in 2020, so even if we'd had a normal season, we'd have likely seen 2019's record of 1,410 players on MLB rosters broken. But due to the pandemic, rosters started the year at 30 and were cut to only 28. Add multiple COVID-19 absences and the revolving door caused by poor starts by hitters and a rash of pitcher arm injuries, and 1,289 players appeared in MLB games in 2020. The comparable figure over the first 67 days of the 2019 season was 1,109. That 16 percent increase works out to an average of six more players per team in 2020 compared to a similar slice of 2019. A future look back at 2020 rosters will include a lot of unfamiliar names.

Plus became a minus.

In advanced metrics, we adjust batter and pitcher performance for park and league/era variations. A plus sign appended to the end of a measure means that it's adjusted for park and league. It's scaled to an average of 100, with higher figures above average and lower figures below average. (Similarly, a metric with a minus is also park- and league-adjusted and scaled to 100, with lower values better.) Here at BP, our advanced measure of offensive performance is DRC+. Baseball-Reference has OPS+ and FanGraphs has wRC+.

Using park and league adjustments, we can compare Dante Bichette's 1995 Steroid Era season at pre-humidor Coors Field (.340/.364/.620, 40 homers, 128 RBI, MVP runner-up) with Jim Wynn's 1968 Year of the Pitcher season at the cavernous Astrodome (.269/.376/.474, 26 homers, 67 RBI, no MVP votes). It's not close. DRC+, OPS+, and wRC+ all give the nod to Wynn, handily. This is a useful tool. As my Baseball Prospectus colleague Patrick Dubuque tweeted last fall, "Please note that when I ask how you are, I am already adjusting for era."

The 2020 season messes up plus (and minus) stats for two reasons. First, the park adjustment was based on only 30 home games instead of the usual 81. Everything noted above regarding the short season applies, literally doubly, to park effect calculations. DRC+ uses a single-season park factor. OPS+ uses a three-year average and wRC+ five years. The figure for 2020 is suspect.

Second, OPS+ and wRC+ adjust for league: American and National. (DRC+ adjusts for opponent, regardless of league.) While there were two leagues in 2020, they were an artificial construct. To reduce travel, teams played opponents geographically, not based on league. There weren't two leagues, American and National. There were three, Western, Central, and Eastern.

That makes a difference because teams in the same league played in different run-scoring environments. AL teams scored 4.58 runs per game, NL teams 4.71. That's a small difference. But teams in the East scored 0.21 more runs per game (4.95) than teams in the West (4.74), and they both scored a lot more than Central teams (4.25). Adjusting for league misses that difference, so this book will be safe in that regard, but other sources may be distorted somewhat.

Not every game was a "game."
In 2020, the rising tide of strikeouts was finally stemmed. Strikeouts per team per game fell from 8.8 in 2019 to 8.7 in 2020. That marked the first decline after 14 straight annual increases.

In 2020, the rising tide of strikeouts rose higher. Batters struck out in 23.4 percent of plate appearances compared to 23.0 percent in 2019. That marked the 15th straight annual increase.

Both are true statements.

Because of two rule changes—seven-inning doubleheaders and runners on second in extra innings—games in 2020 were unprecedented in their brevity. There were 37.0 plate appearances per game in 2020. The only years with fewer were 1904 and 1906-1909. The average game in 2020 entailed 8.61 innings pitched, the fewest since 1899.

So when you see any per-game stats for 2020, you need to increase them by 3 or 4 percent to get them on equal footing with recent years.

Or, better, just ignore them. Last year happened. There were major league games contested between major league teams. But when you're looking at those physical or electronic baseball cards, when you're weaving narratives over why this young player's inevitable rise to stardom fell apart or why that old veteran rekindled his magic, don't linger on the 2020 line. It was just too weird.

Thanks to Lucas Apostoleris for research assistance.

—*Rob Mains is an author of Baseball Prospectus.*

Tranches of WAR

by Russell A. Carleton

We ask "replacement level" to be a lot of things. Sometimes contradictory things. Sometimes I wonder if we know what it even means anymore. The original idea was that it represented the level of production that a team could expect to get from "freely available talent", including bench players, minor leaguers, and waiver wire pickups. It created a common benchmark to compare everyone to, and for that reason, it represented an advancement well beyond what was available at the time. In fact, it created a language and a framework for evaluating players that was not just better but *entirely* different than what came before it.

But then we started mumbling in that language. The idea behind "wins above replacement" was one part sci-fi episode and one part mathematical exercise. Imagine that a player had disappeared before the season and suddenly, in an alternate timeline, his team would have had to replace him. The distance between him and that replacement line was his value. We need to talk about that alternate timeline.

Without getting too into 2:00 am "deep conversations" with extensive navel-gazing, it's worth thinking about why one player might not be playing, while another might.

- A player might not be playing because he has a short-term injury or his manager believes that he needs a day off.
- A player might not be playing because he has a longer-term injury that requires him to be on the injured list.

There's a difference here between these two situations. In particular, the first one generally *doesn't* involve a compensatory roster move, while the second one does. It's possible, though not guaranteed, that the person who will be replacing the injured/resting player would be the same in either case. That matters. Teams generally carry a spare part for all eight position players on the diamond, although in the era of a four-player bench, those spare parts usually are the backup plan for more than one spot.

Cleveland 2021

A couple of years ago, I posed a hypothetical question. Suppose that a team had two players in its system fighting for a fourth outfielder spot. One of them was a league average hitter, but would be worth 20 runs below average if allowed to play center field for a full season. One of them was a perfectly average fielder, but would be 15 runs below average as a hitter, if allowed to play an entire season. Which of the two should the team roster? It's tempting to say the second one, as overall, he is the better player. That misses the point. A league average hitter on the bench isn't just a potential replacement for an injured outfielder. He might also pinch hit for the light-hitting shortstop in a key spot. You keep the average hitter on the roster, even though he isn't a hand-in-glove fit for one specific place on the field, because being a bench player is a different job description than being a long-term fill-in for someone. If you find yourself in need of a longer-term fill-in, you can bring the other guy up from AAA.

When we're determining the value of an everyday player though, if he had disappeared before the season and a team would have had to replace his production, they likely would have done it with a player who was a long-term fill-in type because they would have had to replace a guy who played everyday. Maybe that's the same guy that they would have rostered on their bench anyway, but we don't know. It gets to the query of what we hope to accomplish with WAR. Are we looking for an accurate modeling of reality or are we looking for a common baseline to compare everyone to? Both have their uses, but they are somewhat different questions.

Let's talk about another dichotomy.

- A player might not be playing because he isn't very good and is a bench-level player.
- A player might not be playing because there is another player on the team who has a situational advantage that makes him the better choice today. The classic case of this is a handedness platoon. On another day, he might be a better choice.

When we think about player usage, I think we're still stuck in the model that there are starters and there are scrubs. We have plenty of words for bench players or reserves or backups or utility guys. We do still have the word "platoon" in our collective vocabulary, but in the age of short benches, it's hard to construct one. It's always been hard to construct them. You have to find two players who hit with different hands, have skill sets that complement each other, and probably play the same position. In the era of the short bench, one of them had probably better double as a utility player in some way. Baseball has a two-tiered language geared toward the idea of regulars and reserves. The fact that it was so easy for me to find plenty of synonyms for "a player whose primary function is to come into a game to replace a regular player if he is injured or resting" should tell you something.

I'm always one to look for "unspoken words" in baseball. What is it called when someone is both half of a platoon and the utility infielder? That guy exists sometimes, but he reveals himself in that role—usually by accident. We don't have a word for that, and whenever I find myself saying "we don't have a word for that", I look for new opportunities. What do you call it, further, when the job of being the utility infielder is decentralized across the whole infield with occasional contributions from the left fielder? It's not even a "super-utility" player. What happens when you build your entire roster around the idea that everyone will be expected to be a triple major?

⚾ ⚾ ⚾

I think someone else beat me to this one, and on a grand scale. Platoons work because we know that hitters of the opposite hand to the pitcher get better results than hitters of the same hand, usually to the tune of about 20 points of OBP. If you want to express that in runs, it usually comes out to somewhere around 10 to 12 runs of linear weights value prorated across 650 PA. But hang on a second, now let's say that we have two players who might start today, both of roughly equal merit with the bat. One has a handedness advantage, but is the worse fielder of the two. In that case, as long as his "over the course of a season" projection as a fielder at whatever position you want to slot him into is less than a 10-run drop from the guy he might replace, then he's a better option today.

We're not used to thinking of utility players as bat-first options, who would play below-average defense at three different infield positions. That guy might hook on as a 2B/3B/LF type (Howie Kendrick, come on down!) but teams usually think to themselves that they need as their utility infielder someone who "can handle" shortstop, the toughest of the infield spots to play. If someone can do that *and* hit well, he's probably already starting somewhere, so he's not available as a utility infielder. It's easier for those glove guys to find a job. In a world where the replacement for a shortstop *has to be* the designated utility infielder, that makes sense.

But as we talked about last week, we're living in a different world. The rate at which a replacement for a regular starter turns out to be *another starter* shifting over to cover has gone way up over the last five years. There was always some of it in the game, but this has been a supernova of switcheroos. Now if your second baseman is capable of playing a decent shortstop, that 2B/3B/LF guy can swap in. He's not actually playing shortstop, and maybe the defense suffers from the switch, but if he's got enough of a bat, he might outhit those extra fielding miscues. And in doing so, he is effectively your backup shortstop.

Somewhere along the lines, teams got hip to the idea of multi-positional play from their regulars. I've written before about how you can't just put a player, however athletic, into a new position and expect much at first. The data tell us that. Eventually, players can learn to be multi-positionalists, but it takes time, roughly on the order of two months, before they're OK. But there's a hidden message in there. If you give a player some reps at a new spot, he's a reasonably gifted athlete and somewhat smart and willing to learn, he could probably pick it up enough to get to "good enough," and it doesn't take forever. You just have to be purposeful about it. Maybe you get to the point where you can start to say "he's still below average but we could move him there and get another bat into the lineup, and it's a net win."

Teams have started to build those extra lessons into their player development program. It used to be seen as a mark of weakness to be relegated to "utility player" because that meant that you were a bench player (all those synonyms above come with a side of stigma). Now, it's a way of building a team. If you get a few reps in the minors (where it doesn't count) at a spot, you'll have at least played the spot at game speed before. There are limits to how far you can push that. A slow-footed "he's out in left field because we don't have the DH" guy is never going to play short, but maybe your third baseman can try second base and not look like a total moose out there.

⚾   ⚾   ⚾

Back to WAR. I'd argue that the world of starters and scrubs is slowly disintegrating, for good cause. In the event that a regular starter really does go down with an injury–ostensibly, the alternate universe scenario that WAR is attempting to model–it makes the team a little more resilient to replacing him. And the good news is that you're more likely to be able to replace him with the best of the bench bunch, rather than the third-best guy, because the best guy doesn't have to be an exact positional match for the guy who got hurt. And that's what the manager would want to do. He'd want to replace that long-term production, not with an amalgam of everyone else who played that position, but with the best guy available from his reserves.

Now this is still WAR. We still want to retain the principle that we should be measuring a player, and not his teammates. We need some sort of common baseline, and despite what I just said, we'll still need some sort of amalgam. To construct that, I give to you the idea of the tranche. The word, if you've not heard it before, refers to a piece of a whole that is somehow segmented off. It's often used in finance to talk about layers of a financial instrument.

Here, I want you to consider that there are 30 starters at each of the seven non-battery positions (catchers should have their own WAR, since only a catcher can replace a catcher). We can identify them by playing time, and we can futz around with the definition a little bit if we need to. Next, among those who aren't in that starting pool, we identify the top tranche of the 30 best bench players, which I would again identify by playing time, and then the second and third and fourth and so on. If a player were to disappear, his manager would probably want to take a guy from that top tranche of the bench to replace him. In a world where even the starters can slide around the field, that becomes more feasible.

We can take a look at that top tranche and say "How many of them showed that they are able to play (first, second, etc.)?" and therefore could have directly substituted for the starter? How many of them could have been a direct substitute for our injured player? We don't know whether one of them would be on *a specific* team, but we can say that 40 percent of the time, a manager would have been able to draw from tranche 1 in filling the role, and 35 percent from tranche 2. But on tranche 1, we can also look at how many of those players played a position that could have then shifted and covered for that spot. We'd need some eligibility criteria for all of this (probably a minimum number of games played) but it would just be a matter of multiplication. Shortstop would be harder to fill, and managers would probably be dipping a little further down in the talent pool, and so replacement level would be lower, as it is now.

Doing some quick analysis, I found that the difference in just batting linear weights (haven't even gotten into running or fielding) between tranche 1 and tranche 2 in 2019 was about 6.5 runs, prorated across 650 PA. Between tranche 1 and tranche 3, it's 10.8 runs. The ability to shift those plate appearances up the ladder has some real value.

This part is important. We can also give credit to starters for the positions that they showed an ability to play, even if they didn't play them (this is the guy fully capable of playing center, but who's in a corner because the team already has a good center fielder) because he allows a team to carry a player who hits like a left fielder to functionally be the team's backup center fielder. He facilitates that movement upward among the tranches. We can start to appreciate the difference between a left fielder who would never be able to hack it in center (and the compensatory move that his team would have to make) and the left fielder who could do it, but just didn't have to very often.

Past that, you can continue to use whatever hitting and fielding and running metrics you like to determine a player's value, but when we get down to constructing that baseline, I'd argue we need a better conceptual and mathematical framework. It's going to require some more #GoryMath than we're used to, but I'd argue it's a better conceptualization of the way that MLB actually plays the game in 2020. If…y'know…MLB plays in 2020. If WAR is going to be our flagship statistic among the *acronymati*, then we need to acknowledge that it contains some old and starting-to-be-out-of-date assumptions about the game. We may need to tinker with it. Here's my idea for how.

—*Russell A. Carleton is an author of Baseball Prospectus.*

Secondhand Sport

by Patrick Dubuque

Back before time stopped, I liked to go to thrift stores. Now that I'm older, I rarely ever buy anything—I don't need much in my life, now—but I still enjoy the old familiar circuit: check to see if there are baseball cards to write about, look for board or card games to play with the kids, scan for random ironic jerseys, hit the book section. It takes ten, maybe fifteen minutes. Thrift stores are the antithesis of modern online shopping, because you don't know what they have, and you don't even really know what you want. It's junk, literal junk, stuff other people thought was worthless. That's what makes it great.

In an idealized economy, thrift stores shouldn't exist. Everybody has a living wage, and every product has a durability that exactly matches its desired life; nothing should need to be given away, no one should need to be given to. But then, thrift stores shouldn't work on a customer experience level, either. You wouldn't think an ethos of "let's make everything disorganized and hard to find" would lead to customer satisfaction, but low-budget retailers like TJ Maxx and Ross thrive on this model. People like bargain hunting as much for the hunting as the bargain; it's part of the experience, spending time as if it's a wager. There's a thrill, occasionally, in inefficiency.

In sports, the modern overuse of the word "inefficiency" is a condemnation: It insinuates that there is *an* efficiency, a correct way to be found, and that all other ways are wrong ways. It's prevalent in baseball but hardly contained to it; the lifehack, the Silicon Valley disruption are other examples of productivity creep in our daily lives. Their modern success makes plenty of sense. Maximization of resources, after all, is its own puzzle, and an industry of European board games is founded upon it. It's fun to take a system and optimize it, unravel it like a sudoku puzzle. If there's only one kind of genius, after all, there's no way anyone can fail to appreciate it.

Baseball has been hacking away at these perceived inefficiencies since its inception: platoons, bullpens, farm systems were all installed to extract more out of the tools at hand. But it's been a particular badge of the sabermetric movement, from Ken Phelps and his All-Star Team to Ricardo Rincon and the darlings of *Moneyball*. It's business, but it's also an ethos: the idea that there's treasure among the trash, something we all failed to appreciate until someone brought it to light.

It's the myth that made Sidd Finch so enticing, that fuels so many "best shape" narratives and new pitch promises. We all, athletes and unathletic sportswriters, want to believe that there's genius trapped inside us, and that it's just a matter of puzzling out the combination to unlock it. That our art, our style is the next inefficiency, waiting for our own Billy Beane. It's why we root for underdogs, and why we're excited for the Mike Tauchmans and the Eurubiel Durazos, champions of skin-deep mediocrity.

Except we aren't anymore, really. The days of "Free X" have descended beyond the ring of irony and into obscurity. There are still Xs to be freed, or at least one X, duplicated endlessly: Mike Ford, Luke Voit, Max Muncy. The undervalued one-dimensional slugger demonstrated how the game hasn't quite culturally caught up to its logical extreme. But for those who don't fit the rather spacious mold, times are grimmer. As Rob Arthur revealed several months ago, there's been a marked increase in the number of sub-replacement relievers. It's the outcome of a greater number of teams forced to play out games without the talent to win them, but it's also emblematic of the modern tendency of teams to dispose of their disposable assets, burning through cost-controlled arms the way that man chopped down forests in *The Lorax*. Stuff just isn't built to outlive their original owners anymore.

It's unsurprising, given how well-mined the market for inefficiencies has been of late. The disciples of the early analytics departments, and the disciples of those, have proliferated the league, with only a few backwater holdouts. The league has grown smarter, but every team has learned the same lesson. In fact, the phenomenon creates a peculiar kind of feedback loop: As teams value a specific subset of players or skills, prospective athletes learn to increase their own marketability by conforming themselves to the demands of their prospective employers.

And that's tragic, in the way that the extinction of animals is tragic; a certain amount of biodiversity in baseball has been lost. Shortstops hit like outfielders. Pitchers don't hit at all. Only the catchers remain idiosyncratic, thanks to the defensive demands of their position; eventually they too will be required to produce like everyone else, or they'll meet the fate of their battery mates. A perfect economy requires perfect production.

I mentioned earlier that more and more, I leave thrift stores empty-handed. It is true that I am more discerning than in the past; my bookshelves are full, and there are more streaming films than I will ever be able to watch. But there are other factors at play.

Thrift stores are, in a way, the bond markets of retail. When the economy is rough and other retailers are struggling, more people look secondhand for their products. But as recently as last year, publications were noting a reversal of the trend: Companies like Goodwill and Savers were expanding despite a strong economy. Publications credited a heightened sense of environmentalism and a rejection of cutting-edge fashion as drivers behind the increase, though the more likely answer is the modern American economy hasn't showered its favors equally, particularly among the young.

But it is more than just the economy. Baseball and thrift stores share something else in common, evident in our current conversations about re-starting the sport: They live in the gray area between public service and private enterprise. Thrift stores provide affordable necessities to lower-class citizens, and collectibles and fashion for the middle-class. Because of the success of the latter, prices have gone up across the board. Especially in terms of clothing, the middle-class flight from fashion into vintage has instead carried the aftereffects of fashion, including its costs, into a territory where people just want clothes. But there's another factor in the rise of prices, in the form of the internet.

The Goodwills of the world have grown smarter, too, employing the internet to extract full value from their detritus. Ebay, similarly, has lost much of the charm it had as a new frontier around the turn of the century. Everything has a price point now; even individual taste is no match for the algorithm, because anything rare, no matter how niche its market, is a collectible to someone.

The internet has had the same effect on thrift stores that sabermetrics has had on baseball; its equivalent to OBP was the bar scanner. As detailed in Slate, the rise of second-party stores on eBay and Amazon birthed an entire industry of used-good salespeople, armed with PDAs and scanners, buying books for three dollars to sell online for five. The author, Michael Savitz, reports earning $60,000 by working nearly 80 hours a week; he makes it clear that this is not a vocation of his choosing. It's long hours, with no real creativity or individuality, skimming the cream off of a local establishment and flipping it to someone with a little more money on the other side of the country. And once the vocation exists, the obvious question arises: why wait to put the wares out on the shelves? Why allow value to exist at all?

Nothing is ruined. Thrift stores will continue to sell polo shirts and DVDs, and baseball will continue to exist and make or lose money, depending on who you believe. But as we continue to refine our knowledge, we lose something in the conquest for efficiency, a delight born out of the unknown. The problem isn't the efficiency itself; we can't blame the booksellers, or the people sweeping freeways to collect grams of platinum from damaged catalytic converters. The problem is a system that requires this sort of profit-skimming behavior in order to feed families (or, for corporations, maximize shareholder return).

Cleveland 2021

In times like these, with the 2020 season on the brink and the collective bargaining agreement close behind, it can often feel like the current situation is untenable. It can't keep going like this, even if we don't know what to do about it. But as with thrift stores, there's an equally irresistible feeling that it *has* to keep going, that it would be unimaginable to not have this broken, amazing sport. Both industries exist on an invisible foundation of friction, of chaos and unpredictability, even as both see their foundations buffed down to a perfect, untouchable polish. But if COVID-19 and its financial ramifications do, as some have suggested, make it such that the baseball that returns is fundamentally different than the baseball that came before, perhaps this is the time to lean in, and change the game even more. Fix bunting. Make defense more difficult. Create viable, alternate strategies. Add some chaos back into baseball. It's fun when no one knows quite where things are.

—Patrick Dubuque is an author of Baseball Prospectus.

Steve Dalkowski Dreaming

by Steven Goldman

We dream of being a pitcher, of starring in the major leagues. Depending on your age and your sense of historical perspective, you might imagine yourself as Walter Johnson, throwing harder than anyone else—hitting more batters than anyone else, too, but always feeling bad about it. You could picture yourself as a Tom Seaver or a David Cone, with all the stuff in the world but still being cerebral about it, thinking about so much more than burning 'em in there. There are so many models one could choose: You could be a Lefty Gomez, Jim Bouton, or Bill Lee, skilled, but not taking the whole thing too seriously, or a Lefty Grove, Bob Gibson, or Steve Carlton, powerful but treating each start like a mission to be survived instead of a game to be enjoyed.

Very few would dream of being Steve Dalkowski, the former Baltimore Orioles prospect who died of COVID-19 last week at the age of 80. Yet, there is something just as noble in Dalkowski's negative accomplishments—and accomplishments is what they are—as there is in the precision-engineered pitching of a Greg Maddux. You have to be very good to be that bad. Dalkowski had all of the stuff of the greatest pitchers but none of the command; his story is not one of failing to conquer his limitations, but striving against one of the cruelest hands that fate or genetics or personality can deal us: A desire to achieve great things which is almost but not quite matched by the ability to meet that goal.

As with Johnson, Grove, Bob Feller, and the rest of the hard-throwing pitchers who played before the advent of modern radar guns, we have to take the word of the players and coaches who saw Dalkowski pitch as to his velocity. He was a hard-drinking, maximum-effort pitcher who, if their memories are to be believed, consistently threw over 100 miles per hour. His was the Maltese Fastball, the stuff that dreams are made of. The problem is that velocity without command and control is still a good distance from utility. Dalkowski was the most effective towel you could design for a fish, the sleekest bathing suit intended to be worn by an astronaut, but that doesn't mean he wasn't beautiful: We can appreciate a journey even if it doesn't end at the intended destination.

Whether because of sloppy mechanics he couldn't calm, an inability to understand that a consistent 98 in the strike zone would likely be more effective than a consistent 110 out of it, or all that beer, Dalkowski could never make the adjustments that pitchers like Feller and Nolan Ryan made before him, possibly because he had so far to go: Feller, who never pitched in the minors, came up at 17 and spent three years walking almost seven batters per nine innings before settling in at 3.8 beginning when he was 20. Ryan started out walking over six batters per nine but gradually improved as his long career played out; for him to go from 6.2 walks per nine with the 1966 Greenville Mets to 3.7 with the 1989 Texas Rangers represents a 40 percent reduction. An equivalent improvement by Dalkowski would still have left him walking over 11 batters per nine innings.

Dalkowski was like *The Room* of pitchers, a player so bad he became good again. Cal Ripken, Sr., who both played with and managed Dalkowski, recalled in a 1979 *Sporting News* "where are they now" piece the occasion when the pitcher crossed up his catcher and his fastball, "hit the plate umpire smack in the mask. The mask broke all to pieces and the umpire wound up in the hospital for three days with a concussion. If they ever had a radar gun in those days, I'll bet Dalkowski would have been timed at 110 miles an hour."

Signed by the Orioles out of New Britain High in Connecticut in 1957, Dalkowski was sent to Kingsport in the Appalachian League, where he pitched 62 innings. He allowed only 22 hits in 62 innings, or 3.2 per nine, a number with no equivalent in major league history (though Aroldis Chapman came close in 2014), and also struck out 121 (17.6 per nine) and walked 129 (18.7). He was also charged with 39 wild pitches. That June, one of his fastballs clipped a Dodgers prospect named Bob Beavers and carried away part of his ear. "The first pitch was over the backstop, the second pitch was called a strike, I didn't think it was," Beavers said last year. "The third pitch hit me and knocked me out, so I don't remember much after that. I couldn't get in the sun for a while, and I never did play baseball again." Former minor leaguer Ron Shelton based the *Bull Durham* pitcher Nuke LaLoosh on Dalkowski. And yet, to see him as a figure of fun, an amusing loser, is to misunderstand something unique and strange.

Dalkowski kept on posting some of the strangest lines in baseball history. Pitching for the Stockton Ports of the Class C California League in 1960, he struck out 262 and walked 262 in 170 innings. Yet, he did improve, especially after pitching for Earl Weaver at Elmira in 1962. Weaver had previously had Dalkowski at Aberdeen in 1959, but wasn't ready to grapple with him then. This time he was. "I had grown more and more concerned about players with great physical abilities who could not learn to correct certain basic deficiencies no matter how much you instructed or drilled them," he related in his autobiography, *It's What You Learn After You Know It All That Counts*. He got permission from the Orioles to give all of his players the Stanford-Binet IQ test. "Dalkowski finished in the 1 percentile in his ability to understand facts. Steve, it was said to say, had the ability to do everything but learn." [sic]

IQ tests are problematic diagnostic tools, so take Weaver's estimate of Dalkowski's mental capabilities with a grain of salt. What's important is that even if he got to the right answer by way of the wrong reason, Weaver had learned something valuable. His insight was to stop asking Dalkowski to learn new pitches and just let him get by with the two that he had. Were Dalkowski a prospect today, that would have been a no-brainer: Can't develop a third pitch? The bullpen is right over there, sir. Player development wasn't like that then, but Weaver, temporarily Dalkowski's mentor, could let him work with what he had. According to Weaver, the pitcher responded: "In the final 57 innings he pitched that season Dalkowski gave up 1 earned run, struck out 110 batters, and walked only 11." It's not true—as per the *Elmira Star-Gazette*, as of late July, Dalkowski had walked 71 in 106 innings and finished with 114 in 160 innings, which means Dalkowski's control actually faded at the end of the season rather than improved—but that doesn't mean it didn't happen in some sense, just that it didn't happen that way. Again, it's the journey, not the destination, and his ERA was 3.04 so *something* had gone right.

Also along the way: The next spring, Orioles manager Billy Hitchcock was rooting for Dalkowski to make the team as a long-man—maybe Weaver had gotten through to him. There were things out of Weaver's control, like the universe's twisted sense of humor: that March, Dalkowski's elbow went "twang."

You sometimes read that it was the Orioles' insistence on Dalkowski learning the curve that did him in, but even if they hadn't learned their lesson, the injury was probably just a coincidence: Dalkowski had thrown an incredible number of pitches over the previous few years. Still, it testifies to the dangers of trying to get what you want and risking the loss of what you had. Dalkowski tried to come back, but the 110-mph stuff was gone. A pitcher with no control and no stuff is…a civilian. What followed were years of vagabond living, arrests for drunkenness. There were Alcoholics Anonymous meetings, assistance from baseball alumni associations, but none of it took. From the 1990s until the time of his passing he dwelt in an assisted living facility, suffering from alcohol-related dementia. He'd been a heavy drinker since his teenage years. As with all those pitches per game, there was a price to be paid. You make choices on the journey and some of them are irrevocable. It's like a fairy tale: "Bite of poison apple? Don't mind if I do."

In the aforementioned *Sporting News* profile, Chuck Stevens, the head of the Association of Professional Ballplayers of America, a ballplayer charity, said, "I've got nothing against drinking. I do it myself sometimes. But, I don't condone common drunkenness. We went through lots of heartache and many dollars, but Dalkowski didn't want to help himself and we weren't going to keep him drunk." The journey is *un*like a fairy tale: No one will come along and kiss it better, not if they're busy forming judgments.

In the end, we are left with a sort of philosophical chicken/egg conundrum: Is failing to meet your goals evidence of unfulfilled potential or the lack of it? Isn't what you did by definition what you were capable of doing? Or could you have broken through to something better with the right help, the right lucky break? These are unanswerable questions, and how we try to answer them may say more about us than about the people we're judging.

No pitcher ever has it easy. *All* pitchers must work hard. *All* pitchers must refine their craft. It's almost never just about *stuff*. Dalkowski dreaming is no insult to the great pitchers who made it; from Pete Alexander to Max Scherzer, they have all earned their way up. And yet, if it is true that we can only do as much as we can do, then the journey would be more of an adventure, the ultimate triumph or defeat more noble, if like Dalkowski we lacked 100 percent of the confidence, the command, the self-possession, the commitment, the resistance to making bad decisions that so many great players possess—to be gloriously human. Or, to put it more succinctly, it would be fun to be able to throw as hard as any person ever has. Even if just for a moment, and even if nothing more came of it than that, no one could say you hadn't lived life to the fullest.

—*Steven Goldman is an author of Baseball Prospectus.*

A Reward For A Functioning Society

by Cory Frontin and Craig Goldstein

On July 5, Nationals reliever Sean Doolittle said in the middle of a press conference regarding the restart of Major League Baseball and what would later be known as summer camp, "sports are like the reward of a functioning society." This sentence was amidst a much longer, thoughtful reply about the societal and health conditions under which MLB players were being brought back. It's a very similar sentiment to one Jane McManus used on April 7, when she discussed the White House's meeting with sports commissioners. She said "sports are the effect of a functioning society—not the precursor."

Both versions of the same sentiment spoke to a laudable ideal in the context of a country that was not addressing a rampaging virus, and opting instead to bring sports back for the feeling of normalcy rather than the reality of it. "Priorities," as McManus said.

On Wednesday, the NBA's Milwaukee Bucks conducted a wildcat/political strike, refusing to come out for Game 5 of their playoff series against the Orlando Magic. The Magic refused to accept the forfeit, and shortly thereafter other playoff series were threatened by player strikes. Eventually the league moved to postpone that day's games, folding to players leveraging their united power.

The backdrop against which these actions took place was the shooting by police of Jacob Blake. Blake was shot in the back seven times by police, as he attempted to get into his vehicle. He managed to survive the assault, but is paralyzed from the waist down.

⚾ ⚾ ⚾

The step taken to walk out, first by the Milwaukee Bucks, then subsequently by other NBA, WNBA, and MLB teams, was a step toward upholding the virtue of the sentiment described by McManus and Doolittle. But that sentiment does not align with the broad history of sports in this and other countries, a history that contradicts the core of the idealistic statement.

Sports have been a significant part of American society for most of its existence, expanding in importance and influence in recent years. The idea that society was functioning in a way that was worthy of the reward of sports for most of that time is laughable. Much of America is not functioning and has not functioned for Black people, full stop. The oppressed people at the center of this political act by players, specifically Black players, in concert throughout the NBA and in fits and starts throughout Major League Baseball, have not known a society that functions for them rather than *because* of them.

Politics has been part of the sports landscape since the inception of sport, but for just about as long people have bemoaned its presence. Sports are to be an escape, it is said. An escape from what, though? A functioning society?

No, the presence of sports has never signified a cultural or political system that is on the up and up. Rather, the presence of sports *reflect and reinforce the society* that produces them.

⚾   ⚾   ⚾

The Negro Leagues were born out of societal dysfunction. The need for entirely separate leagues, composed of Black and Latino players barred from the Major Leagues because of racism? That is not a functioning society, and yet there were sports.

Even the integration of players from the Negro Leagues resulted in a transfer of power and wealth from Black-owned businesses and communities and into white ones, mirroring the dysfunction that had bled into every aspect of American society at the time. Japheth Knopp noted in the Spring 2016 Baseball Research Journal:

> *The manner in which integration in baseball—and in American businesses generally—occurred was not the only model which was possible. It was likely not even the best approach available, but rather served the needs of those in already privileged positions who were able to control not only the manner in which desegregation occurred, but the public perception of it as well in order to exploit the situation for financial gain. Indeed, the very word integration may not be the most applicable in this context because what actually transpired was not so much the fair and equitable combination of two subcultures into one equal and more homogenous group, but rather the reluctant allowance—under certain preconditions—for African Americans to be assimilated into white society.*

To understand the value of a movement, though, is not to understand how it is co-opted by ownership, but to know the people it brings together and what they demand. When Jackie Robinson—the player who demarcated the inevitability of the end of the Negro leagues—attended the March on Washington for Jobs and Freedom in 1963, he did so with his family and marched alongside the people. He stood alongside hundreds of thousands to fight for their common civil and labor rights. "The moral arc of the universe is long," many freedom fighters have echoed, "but it bends towards justice." The bend, it is less frequently said, happens when a great mass of people place the moral arc of the universe on their knee and apply force, as Jackie, his family, and thousands of others did that day.

⚾ ⚾ ⚾

Of course, taking the moral arc of the universe down from the mantle and bending it is not without risk. Perhaps the outsized influence of athletes is itself a mark of a dysfunctional society, but, nonetheless, hundreds of athletes woke up on Wednesday morning with the power to bring in millions of dollars in revenues. That very power, as we would come to find out, was matched with the equal and opposite power to *not* bring those revenues. That power, in hands ranging from the Milwaukee Bucks, to Kenny Smith in the *Inside the NBA* Studio, from the unexpected ally, Josh Hader, and his largely white teammates to the notably Black Seattle Mariners, would be exercised for a single demand: the end to state violence against Black people. Not unlike the March itself, it sat at the intersection of the civil rights of Black Americans and bold labor action. The March on Washington stood in the face of a false notion of integration—against an integration of extraction but not one of equality—and proposed something different. Just the same, the acts of solidarity of August 26, 2020 will be remembered in stark defiance of MLB's BLM-branded, but ultimately empty displays on opening weekend.

Bold defiance like this can never be without risk. By choosing to exercise this power, the Milwaukee Bucks took a risk. They risked vitriol and backlash from those they disagreed with. They risked fines or seeing their contracts voided, as a walkout like this is prohibited by their CBA. They risked forfeiting a playoff game, one that, as the No. 1 seed in the playoffs, they'd worked all year to attain. They didn't know how Orlando would respond. It wasn't clear that other teams throughout the league would follow suit in solidarity. And it wasn't known the league would accept these actions and moderately co-opt them by "postponing" games that would have featured no players.

If the league reschedules the games, some of the athletes' risk—their shared sacrifice—will be diminished, in retrospect. But they did not know any of that when they took that risk. And it is often left to athletes to take these risks when others in society won't, especially those of their same socioeconomic status and levels of influence.

It is athletes, specifically BIPOC athletes, that take them, though, because they live with the risk of being something other than white in this country every day. They are no strangers to the realities of police brutality. It seems incongruous then, to say that sports are a reward for a functioning society when we rely on athletes to lead us closer to being a functioning society. Luckily, our beloved athletes, WNBA players first and foremost among them, understand what sports truly are: a pipebender for the moral arc of the universe.

—Craig Goldstein is editor in chief of Baseball Prospectus. Cory Frontin is an author of Baseball Prospectus.

Index of Names

Allen, Logan 79
Arias, Gabriel 62, 87
Bauers, Jake 63
Bieber, Shane 36
Bracho, Aaron 91
Bradley, Bobby 64
Burns, Tanner 80, 92
Cantillo, Joey 80, 93
Chang, Yu 65
Civale, Aaron 38
Clase, Emmanuel 81, 92
Espino, Daniel 81, 88
Freeman, Mike 66
Freeman, Tyler 67, 90
Gamel, Ben 16
Giménez, Andrés 18
Hamilton, Billy 68
Hankins, Ethan 82, 89
Hedges, Austin 20
Hembree, Heath 40
Hentges, Sam 82
Hernandez, Cesar 22
Hill, Cam 42
Johnson, Daniel 68, 94
Jones, Nolan 69, 86
Karinchak, James 44
Luplow, Jordan 24
Martin, Leonys 70
Maton, Phil 46
McKenzie, Triston 48, 86
Mercado, Oscar 71
Miller, Owen 72, 93
Naquin, Tyler 72
Naylor, Bo 73, 93
Naylor, Josh 74
Parker, Blake 50
Pérez, Oliver 52
Pérez, Roberto 26
Plesac, Zach 54
Plutko, Adam 56
Puig, Yasiel 75
Quantrill, Cal 58
Ramírez, José 28
Reyes, Franmil 30
Rocchio, Brayan 76, 89
Rosario, Amed 32
Rosario, Eddie 34
Santana, Domingo 76
Torres, Lenny 93
Tucker, Carson 77, 91
Valera, George 77, 85
Wittgren, Nick 60
Zimmer, Bradley 78

For the Joy of Keeping Score

THIRTY81 Project is an ongoing graphic design project focused on the ballparks of baseball. Since being established in 2013, scorecards have been a fundemantal part of the effort. Each two-page card is uniquely ballpark-centric — there are 30 variants — and designed with both beginning and veteran scorekeepers in mind. Evolving over the years with suggestions from fans, broadcasters, and official scorers, the sheets are freely available to everyone as printable letter-size PDFs at the project webshop: www.THIRTY81Project.com

Download, Print, Score, Repeat …

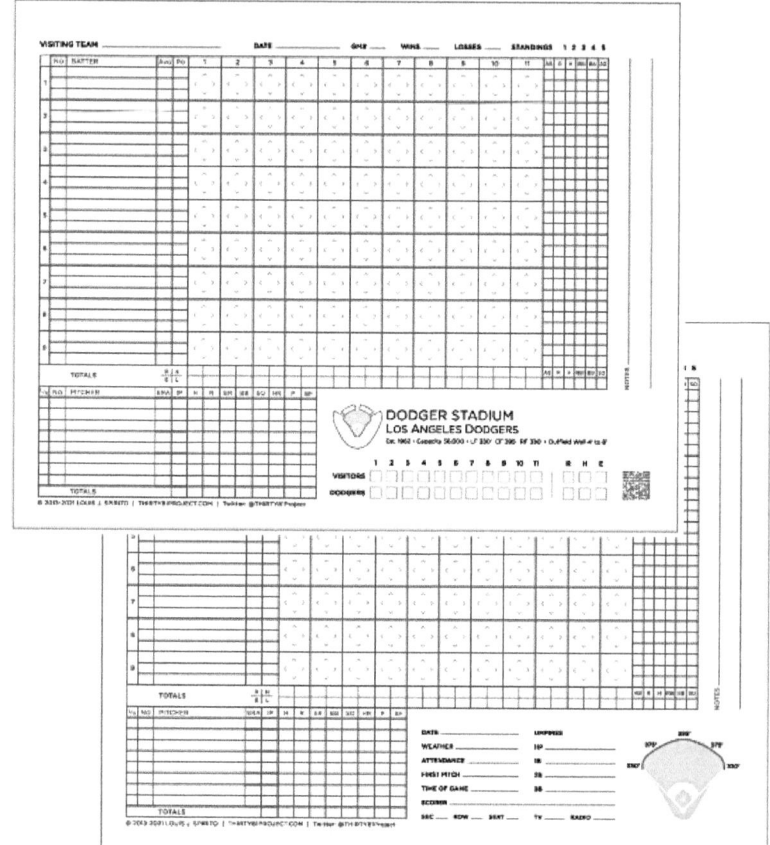

Scorecard design ©2013-2021 Louis J. Spirito | THIRTY81Project